THE POETRY OF
ERNEST DOWSON

THE

POETRY

OF

ERNEST DOWSON

EDITED,

WITH AN INTRODUCTION

BY

DESMOND FLOWER

RUTHERFORD • MADISON • TEANECK
FAIRLEIGH DICKINSON UNIVERSITY PRESS

THE POETRY OF ERNEST DOWSON.
Introduction and Notes Copyright 1934, 1950
and © Desmond Flower 1967.
First American edition published 1970 by
Associated University Presses, Inc.
Cranbury, New Jersey 08512

Library of Congress Catalogue Card Number: 75-88560

ISBN: 0-8386-7551-4
Printed in the United States of America

CONTENTS

Contents

DECORATIONS

IN VERSE

Contents

IN PROSE

HITHERTO UNPUBLISHED POEMS

Contents

Contents

INTRODUCTION

T HAT "distance lends enchantment" is a hoary truth which has at last been justified in the extraordinary 'nineties. A variety of reasons, of which envy was perhaps not the least, invested the memory of that remarkable decade with an undeserved stigma of ineffective wickedness. But in recent years a great deal has been written concerning the broken lives, the unhappy, early, suicidal deaths of many of the writers of the 'nineties; and many inferences have been drawn from their despair. The most usual, and perhaps the most erroneous, is that had Lionel Johnson, Ernest Dowson, John Davidson or Hubert Crackanthorpe lived, say, in the English Renaissance, they would have written works of an entirely different calibre—on a plane with Tasso or Pascal, as one critic suggests. But is that inference true? It certainly deserves consideration.

No one will deny the glory and importance of Elizabeth's reign in English literature—an age which enjoyed the full flowering of Renaissance splendour in this country. Yet there were few factors to encourage writers then that were not present in the 'nineties, and, indeed, the two periods present such striking similarities that it is odd that instead of being contrasted they have not been more frequently compared. The most obvious similarity is the early death of the gifted writers in both ages. We may assume that it would have done the unfortunate young men of the 'nineties little good to have lived three hundred years before, since their tale of woe is by no means greater than that of Oriana's poets: Marlowe was killed in a brawl, after a day's drinking, at twenty-nine; Greene wasted six years in riotous living, thereafter starved in an attic and died in penury at thirty-four; Peele suffered a discreditable death at thirty-nine after a roistering life; Kyd survived a life of hardship varied with imprisonment for thirty-six years; Nash enjoyed what he himself described as a "life spent in fantasticall satirisme in whose veines hereof I misspent my spirit and prodigally conspired against good houres" and passed away at thirty-four; while even Shakespeare was dead at fifty-two after some years of indifferent health and a final illness brought on, it is said, by a drinking bout with Drayton and Ben Jonson. There is more to be learnt from this than the conclusion that irregular living and misfortune cannot extinguish genius: the men of the 'nineties, in fact, resembled the Elizabethans on all sides. Both were the rebels, the outcasts of a prosperous commercial age, ruled over by a Queen who cared little for the arts: Victoria has lent her name to unenlightened intolerance, while Elizabeth on her death-bed summed up her lifelong attitude to literature by saying to Harington, her godson, "when thou dost feel creeping time at thy gates, these fooleries will please thee less".

Both primarily were group movements: with the exception of Shakespeare, who would overweight any period, and Marlowe, there are no names in the late sixteenth century that are not mentioned in the same breath with half a dozen others—not as writers without whom English literature would be eternally impoverished, but as men who by their acts, their writings and their creed contributed to the fabric of their age. It is not what the Elizabethans wrote, but the way they wrote it, which is of importance. Both were periods which valued manner rather than matter. It has been stated that "the 'nineties is not a period but a point of view, and many of those who figure largely in the decade itself, since they did not share that point of view, must be excluded";[1]

[1] Osbert Burdett, *The Beardsley Period*, 1925.

and the corollary is that those who lived beyond the fringe of the decade but thought alike must belong to it: thus the 'nineties begin with George Moore's *Confessions of a Young Man* in 1886, while Kipling and Hardy find no place; similarly the Elizabethans include Webster and Ford among their number.

Both periods were an end and not a beginning. Both were wealthy beyond previous dreams of avarice: the Elizabethans plundered America while the Victorians seized Africa; on the one hand the Reformation dwindled into the last age of martyrs and Donne's colourful visions of hell, while on the other *Tract* 90 lived in the wholesale conversion to Rome of all the younger writers. Both periods were weary; the poets of the two ages turned away from life, for the taste of it was sour in their mouths: "Let us admit that in Webster's tragedies there is little faith except in the courage of despair; little hope, except in the rest of death; and a love that brings only unhappiness. . . . And yet most great poetry has looked on human destiny with unconcealed sadness. . . ."[1] Whether they be great or not, the poets of the 'nineties were at no pains to conceal their dissatisfaction with the lot of man, and with mankind himself. The basis of this lack of sympathy with their surroundings was twofold. First, "æsthetic theories and literary cliques, with us (in England), have generally been due to foreign influence":[2] the Elizabethans' debt to Italy is obvious—Shakespeare drew a dozen plots from sources of Italian origin; the 'nineties' debt to France is equally well known. Secondly, the theory of "Art for Art's sake" was eagerly upheld by the whole group; Wilde stated the theme in his brilliant Essays at the opening of the decade, but beyond him, again, was France, and Flaubert with his *mot juste*. It is hardly surprising that this creed should have appealed to men who expected more of life than the undignified scramble after wealth that the Victorians had made of it. Holding to Wilde's statement that "they are the elect to whom beautiful things mean only Beauty", the poets of the 'nineties shunned

[1] F. L. Lucas, *Complete Works of John Webster*, 1927, Vol. I, Introduction.

[2] Jean Stewart, *Poetry in France and England*, 1931.

a society which valued poetry by the altitude of its moral tone and led their lives along paths which they always hoped would push their art further towards its conclusions. In the preceding decades of the century a poet was a member of society who, by profession or by inclination, wrote poetry; in the 'nineties a poet regarded poetry as an anchorite regards his faith: all his actions were undertaken and calculated in relation to it, and he cared nothing for society—and, in consequence, society cared less for him. Tennyson and Browning might retire into their studies to write as a business man would enter his office, and emerge some hours later with the satisfaction of a job well done to join in the social converse of a luncheon party; but the poet of the 'nineties, willingly ostracised, was never off duty, that "most vivid moment" which it was essential to immortalize was never far distant, and his work, for its own sake, assumed proportions that admitted room for little else. This preoccupation with work, both poetry and prose, reawakened a sense of style that has fluctuated through literary history, but was most prominent with the Elizabethans: "There is no necessary difference in artistic value between a good poem about a flower in the hedge and a good poem about the scent in a sachet"[1]—but it must be a good poem, well written. Webster never troubled to adjust the relationships between his characters—it was of no importance, because what the audience came to the theatre for was a good play in good language. Consequently there is hardly an Elizabethan who did not write well, and, in addition, was obviously excited about doing so; and in the same way Oscar Wilde, who knows no master in the art of handling our language, was excited by rich prose, loaded in every rift with ore. When Dorian Gray picked up *A Rebours* he was fascinated because "the style in which it was written was that peculiar jewelled style, vivid and obscure at once, full of *argot* and of archaism, of technical expressions and of elaborate paraphrases. . . . There were in it metaphors as monstrous as orchids and as subtle in colour";[2] how justly

[1] Arthur Symons, *Studies in Prose and Verse*, 1904.
[2] Oscar Wilde, *The Picture of Dorian Gray*, 1891.

these words might be applied to the earlier period, of which it has been said that "Erudition became more and more a feature of poetry, and the appeal to primitive observations and emotions less piquant than references to the extraordinary, the violent, and even the unwholesome".[1] Books have been written to prove that Shakespeare was a soldier, a falconer, a lawyer or a painter, simply because he was a master of the style that Dorian Gray admired.

Another of the important effects of this group movement was the sudden appearance of numerous manifestos in the form of periodicals; once more, to find a counterpart for the *Yellow Book*, the *Savoy*, *Hobby Horse*, *Pageant* and *Dome*, it is necessary to go back to *Tottell's Miscellany*, *The Phoenix' Nest*, *The Passionate Pilgrim* and *England's Helicon*.

It seems certain now that, however individual reputations may rise or fall, the general reputation of the 'nineties cannot fail to increase. We are beginning to appreciate that the decade did, as it claimed, approach literature in the manner that has characterized, in the past, the greatest periods, and there are few who would deny that poetry subsequently entered very low waters until the renaissance of the 1930's. But the men of the 'nineties were not fortunate in their time. The Boer War, with its two years of nervousness, with Magersfontein, Colenso, Mafeking and Ladysmith, destroyed what was left of a movement which had already lost many of its protagonists; small as the encouragement was that they had received before, these poets could look for even less at a time when a Union Jack fluttered through every stanza of accepted verse. While Lord Kitchener cleared the Transvaal, English poetry too was swept and garnished.

Ernest Dowson's position in this group has never been in doubt: his was the purest and at the same time the most representative poetic genius that it possessed. In evidence of the first quality Professor Grierson has said that he recognizes in him, in Francis Thompson and in Mr. W. B. Yeats, the "unmistakeable lyrical inspiration";[2] of the second Sir Ifor

[1] Sir Edmund Gosse, *The Jacobean Poets*, 1894.
[2] H. J. C. Grierson, *Lyrical Poetry from Blake to Hardy*, 1928.

Evans states that "he is the poet symbolic of the eighteen-nineties; he is in verse what Beardsley was in pictorial art".[1] In spite of the adverse criticism which his poems, in common with those of his friends, received on their original appearance, there seems no reason to doubt that his reputation will rise as high as that of the literary age in which he lived.

Ernest Christopher Dowson was born at Lee, now part of the vast suburbs that spread indefinitely about the main road from London to Folkestone, on August 2nd, 1867. His father, Alfred Dowson, was the owner of Bridge Dock, Lime-house, a small dry dock which survives to-day only as the meagre entrance to an insignificant canal. At that time it had been in the Dowson family for several generations. During the early part of Ernest Dowson's life, Bridge Dock was let, and his father was able to fortify his indifferent health by frequent travels abroad in a warmer climate: journeys on which his son often accompanied him. Father and son were never in one place long enough for Dowson to go regularly to school, but long spells in France, mostly on the Riviera, gave him a thorough command of French, while he managed in addition to pick up a knowledge of Latin and with it a love for the Classics. He went up to Queen's College, Oxford, in 1886, but his first and last attempt at regular education was not a success and he went down the following year with no degree, but a love for Catullus, Propertius, Flaubert, Balzac, Verlaine and Henry James. For a while he lived with his family in Maida Vale, and at Woodford, in Essex; his time was spent writing. He had written poetry from an early age and his first poem that has survived was published by *London Society* in November 1886: it was the *Sonnet to a Little Girl*. Throughout his life, however, he preferred his prose and, indeed, he was always looked upon as a prose writer by his friends until one day he produced for Herbert Horne, then editing the refounded *Hobby Horse* with Selwyn Image, the beautiful *Amor Umbratilis*; it was written in September 1890,

[1] B. Ifor Evans, *English Poetry in the Later Nineteenth Century*, 1933.

and by the same month in the following year he had composed a dozen of his finest verses and was recognized by his friends in the Rhymers' Club as a considerable poet.

As ships coming up the Thames grew bigger and could no longer be squeezed for their repairs into the modest dimensions of Bridge Dock, that concern grew less and less prosperous, until the Company that rented it failed. Alfred Dowson then decided to carry on the unwelcome business himself with the help of his son; but Ernest's heart was not in Limehouse, and as a rule he left early in the afternoon and returned late the next morning from the West End where his literary friends gathered. Matters continued in this way until his father's death in 1894; then he was happy to relinquish Bridge Dock to the foreman and depart for France: whence he seldom returned except for short intervals.

The first four years of the 'nineties were the best of Dowson's life, though the seeds of his misfortunes, so soon to crowd on him, were sown at that time. He moved in the centre of the literary and artistic movement, and this mental stimulus kept him constantly at work: the whole of *Verses* and most of *Decorations* was composed then, the *Pierrot of the Minute* written and produced, *The Comedy of Masks*, in collaboration with Arthur Moore, appeared, and the stories later collected in *Dilemmas* came out in various periodicals. But his lungs were already infected, and, like so many consumptives, he treated his health with reckless disregard. Nothing could have been worse for him than long evenings in the "Crown" and Café Royal, prolonged to all hours because the company was pleasant and the effort of getting home so great, followed often by too few hours of uncomfortable sleep in a friend's armchair before it was time to jolt back to Limehouse on the morning train. By 1896, after two years abroad, he had passed his prime. *Verses* appeared, containing so many glories of his youthful talent, and in spite of adverse reviews the five hundred copies were sold. Leonard Smithers, his publisher, who now began to pay him a salary for all the translating from the French that he could do, visited him fairly often, and several other friends passing through Brittany or

Paris stopped a few days from time to time. But mostly he was alone, and he hated loneliness. He moved on restlessly through France and Belgium, a decrepit figure with a steadily increasing cough:

> *And health and hope have gone the way of love*
> *Into the drear oblivion of lost things.*
> *Ghosts go along with us until the end;*
> *This was a mistress, this, perhaps, a friend.*
> *With pale, indifferent eyes, we sit and wait*
> *For the dropt curtain and the closing gate. . . .*[1]

The only verse that was definitely written after 1896 was in those portions of *La Pucelle* which he did not adapt from the previous translations. When Smithers first projected the publication by his "Lutetia Society" of an English version of Voltaire's satiric epic, it was intended that an entirely new translation should be made. But in the event Dowson put together a skilful patchwork of the existing versions, himself translating where necessary to bridge the gaps. The edition was published in two volumes in 1899. Apart from that, he wrote entirely prose: translations for Smithers, and, erratic as his delivery of it may have been, it cannot be denied that for a sick man he managed to complete a great deal of work. Some friends lost touch, but others wrote regularly; and after Oscar Wilde's departure to France from Reading gaol a warm friendship sprang up between the two exiles. Finally he returned to England and was found in the Euston Road by Mr. R. H. Sherard, who took him to his cottage in Catford. It was a strange fate that brought him back at last to within a short distance of the house in which he was born thirty-three years before: he lived on for six weeks, and then, on February 23rd 1900, he died.

In spite of his position of importance in the 'nineties move-ment, neither Dowson's life nor his works have received much attention; indeed, it is not going too far to say that the facts

[1] *Dregs, Decorations,* 1899.

of his life have been neglected. Estimates of his character and accounts of his life have only been undertaken on three occasions. The first is in Arthur Symons's well-known study which originally appeared as an obituary notice, was then incorporated in a book of essays, and finally became the preface to an edition of Dowson's poems which John Lane published in one volume in 1905. The second is Victor Plarr's *Ernest Dowson, Reminiscences,* 1887-98, which was published in 1914. Plarr, who was Librarian to the Royal College of Surgeons, and moved in most respectable circles, did no more than speak of his own friendship with Dowson. Mr. Symons wrote with all his accustomed skill, though he did not know Dowson so well; in consequence, his criticism of Dowson's poetry is always penetrating and often brilliant, but his biographical details are unreliable and his synthetic Bohemianism led him into performing the greatest disservice to the memory of his friend. To say, for instance, that "there are men whom Dowson's experiences would have made great men, or great writers; for him they did very little", is to express an opinion which it cannot properly assume. The third most recent and most important, is the biography written by Dr. Mark Longaker. Dr. Longaker's enthusiasm and industry brought together a great amount of new material which throws much light on Dowson's life—particularly the tragedy of his parents which must have affected him deeply, and details of his own death. This book also for the first time critically examines the many fragmentary and too often axe-grinding accounts which were written by friends and acquaintances of the poet after his death.[1]

That Dowson's poems met with a bad reception from the Press when they appeared is perhaps hardly surprising: he was not much more fortunate than other poets of the 'nineties. The *Athenæum*, reviewing *Decorations*, remarked that, "after having been ignored or misvalued during his life, he is in some danger of being overestimated simply because he is dead. This second volume of verse, now so sure of being

[1] Mark Longaker, *Ernest Dowson,* 1944, second edition with additional new material, 1945.

respectfully reviewed, is not indeed so good as the first volume, which appeared in 1892 under the title of 'Verses', and was scarcely reviewed at all", and went on to add a comment which explains the low estimate of his poems at that time: "He had neither sustained thought nor sustained passion, but he could set an exquisite moment to music. The music was faint, and did not seize upon the ear by any experimental boldness in the cadence."[1] Even the *Athenæum*, which was sympathetically inclined, could not see that neither sustained thought nor sustained passion were of particular importance in Dowson's work; that he was capable of both is shown by a number of the poems published for the first time in this edition, particularly that to Lady Burton, but what he chose to offer to the public was "verses, in the manner of the French 'symbolists': Verses making for mere sound, and music, with just a suggestion of sense, or hardly that. . . ."[2] Dowson's poems are the quintessence of a quintessence; as one strips an artichoke, he removed leaf after leaf of personal feeling until nothing was left but the core; in an artichoke the core is very succulent—in Dowson's verse there remained a lyric that was the exquisite expression of a personal emotion: "He has removed from his poetry everything except his own narrow circle of sensations. . . ."[3] But the writers of the 'nineties offered their work to a world which expected a message in every line and which delighted in Browning because even he could not recall the meaning of certain things which he had written: before such a public Dowson's exquisite and depressing lucidity was laid at unobservant feet.

It has been stated often enough that Dowson had but few strings to his poetic bow, and it would be idle to deny this. His ill success in love, the unalterable progress from childhood

[1] *Athenæum*, April 12th, 1900.

[2] Unpublished letter to Mr. Arthur Moore, *c.* 1891.

[3] B. Ifor Evans, *Op. cit.* Though I must confess that I cannot agree with Sir Ifor when he continues his sentence, "and these, with the sickening sense of sin that lies behind them, he has tortured himself to express with exquisite perfection." Perfection, yes, but sense of sin, no: surely, rather, sense of regret; une recherche désespérée du temps perdu.

to womanhood of each unsophisticated creature on whom he
set his affections, his disgust with life and mankind when one
of these charming children lived up to his worst fears and
gradually became sex-conscious and gauche, autumn and the
winter of death as the only rest from this *lâcheté*: these, with a
few exceptions which are the more notable for their paucity,
sufficed him.   But from this limited instrument he wrung
every note of which its small compass was capable.   "He
possessed . . . an unusual prosodic skill, not only in the tradi-
tional forms, but in modifications and inventions"[1]—in this
he stands midway between two masters who influenced him
perhaps more directly and more strongly than any others:
Swinburne and Keats.   In his virtuosity he could never equal
"the greatest of metrical conjurors":[2] but that in itself is
nothing, for as Sir Sidney Colvin has pointed out, one of
the landmarks in English verse, Keats' *Poems* of 1817, is
practically a variation on two metres.[3]   Dowson employed
a large number of metres: pentameters in every stanza and
rhyme scheme that he could concoct, a variety of trimeters,
tetrameters and alexandrines.   In the last of these he achieved
his greatest metrical success—the metre of Cynara, which
Sir Ifor Evans has described: "The 'Cynara' poem adds a
new melody to English poetry. . . .   The basic line is the
alexandrine, a line which Dowson particularly admired. He
contrived so to vary the stress and cæsura that all the weari-
ness of the line in English is removed, and there is substituted
a moving lyrical quality.   Dowson's stanza cannot easily be
imitated; the ear that adjusts the licences that bring such
variation has to be nicely attuned."   It is not often in English
that a vintage of such quality comes from the wine-press of
the alexandrine, "the crowning glory of 'classical' French
verse . . . wherein the light fluidity of the language is com-
pensated by length and stateliness of line, and perfect sym-
metry is combined with subtle variation; this point is too often
missed by the foreigner, who raps out the twelve syllables

[1] B. Ifor Evans, *Op. cit.*
[2] Sir Sidney Colvin, *Life of Keats*, 1917.
[3] Sir Sidney Colvin, *ibid.*

and finds (them) . . . monotonous."[1] And, indeed, Dowson was imbued with Gallic taste that was more than a tourist's love of Brittany and went deeper than his Flaubertian passion for the *mot juste* or his successful trifling with the troubadours' metres which Swinburne, Dobson and Bridges had already introduced. He had that true flair for rhythm which, tempered with English lyricism, was in him a supreme virtue, though to French poetry it has so often proved a constricting vice.

Swinburne's legacy to Dowson was one of tone rather than metre: none of the metres that are so characteristic of Swinburne, the *Laus Veneris, Triumph of Time*, and *Ave atque Vale* stanzas, are to be found in the latter's pages (though in *Decorations* there is *Libera Me*, which is little more than an exercise in the style and metre of the *Hymn of Proserpine*), nor is there any attempt at the same metrical *tours de force*: the hendecasyllabics, the sapphics or the double sestinas. But on the other hand there are countless lines which might well have been written by either poet sprinkled through poems which, read in their entirety, admit of no doubt as to their authorship. For it is interesting that, although there are verbal similarities between Swinburne and Dowson which led contemporary critics to sneer at the latter as a mere appendage of The Pines, their outlook and approach in anything more than single lines and occasional stanzas is quite different. Indeed, in this respect Dowson has far more in common with Keats, and frequently a whole passage—as in the obvious case of *Autumnal*, and also the *Sonnet to a Little Girl, No. IV*—has sent me hurrying to the Odes, only to return again with the conclusion that there is nothing more direct than a common approach to a common subject. As Sir Sidney Colvin has said of Keats, Dowson "showed himself from the first one of those chartered borrowers who have the right to draw inspiration as they please";[2] Mr. Edmund Blunden, describing the same characteristic, says that "the verse of Keats . . . is chequered with references to and renova-

[1] Jean Stewart, *Op. cit.*

[2] Sir Sidney Colvin, *Op. cit.*

tions of the detail of earlier men, and furnishes a remarkable opportunity for those who appreciate the art of poetry by itself to exercise their powers. Without going so far as to write of 'the plagiarism of Keats', one may indeed affirm that his poetic habit included, as the means sometimes of inspiration and often of embellishment, the expressions that took his fancy as he read. In this achievement, moreover, there lies no antipathy, but, of course, a tribute to the genius which could assemble (like his own admired Milton in youth) the exquisite and the impressive from the fields of poetry, and command them, rehabilitate them, newly relate them into his own unforgettable achievements."[1] Dowson, too, was a "literary poet" of the same habit, and his work discloses at every turn faint echoes of his wide reading—beside Keats and Swinburne there are poems which have something in common with Horace, Catullus, Propertius, Virgil (the *Eclogues*), Johannes Secundus, Goethe and Verlaine, while the more specific similarity between *Extreme Unction* and a passage in his favourite *Madame Bovary* has been noticed elsewhere.[2]

The number of Dowson's known sonnets has now risen from three to fourteen, which at least entitles him to consideration as a composer in that form, since the total number of Milton's sonnets in English is only eighteen. Of these, two are Shakespearian, and the remaining twelve modelled on one or another of Milton's variations. Crosland in his delightfully pungent manner revelled, not without reason, in exposing Milton's technical shortcomings:[3] the chief of these, a consistent disregard of the Petrarchan rule of the pause, Dowson did not share, for he observed the rule most scrupulously; but it is curious that in half a dozen of his small total he should have employed what Crosland described as "the two worst rhyme-schemes for the conclusion of an English sonnet that it would be possible to arrange", that is to say the c–d–d–c–e–e of the Cromwell, and the c–d–d–c–d–c of the Fairfax sonnet— nor in his hands do they seem so peculiarly wanting. Since

---

[1] Edmund Blunden, *Keats' Ode to a Nightingale* (*London Mercury*).
[2] See p. 258.
[3] T. W. H. Crosland, *The English Sonnet*, 1917.

Keats and Wordsworth, the English sonnet has not been very fortunate in its executants, and the addition of a writer who could keep the rules in the only department of the game where poetry is not a law unto itself,[1] and still compose good poetry is not unimportant.

Dowson's method of poetic composition seems to have been very much the same as that of Keats, as opposed, for instance, to that of Shakespeare, who, according to Ben Jonson, committed his verse to paper in its final form. They were swayed by the mood of the moment, carried away by the idea within them, and lines were written down as they came that the fine flow of inspiration might not be checked by the delay of worrying a phrase into its perfect form. Two good examples of Keats' method are *La Belle Dame Sans Merci*, and the first hundred lines of *Hyperion*: they are full of interesting corrections which show the gradual evolution of the finished lines. There are two examples among Dowson's surviving works that show us the way in which he "got it down somehow", and then hammered the lines into shape. First there is the fragmentary triolet *To think of thee, O death*, which Dowson hurriedly scribbled on a letter to Mr. Arthur Moore and then left: it is so much a fragment, two lines short with even one of the surviving seven no more than a ghost indicated by its first and last word, that I have relegated it to the Notes.[2] Though it can hardly be read with pleasure as poetry, it is an interesting first draft. The second example is *Fantasie Triste*, which is a complete poem, but practically without punctuation and with the rhymes serving as the only link to carry Dowson on to the next line: the result is a first dim outline without any of the compactness which characterized his completed lyrics, and a meandering *morbidezza* which might be taken as a deliberate parody of his own work. Punctuation was important to Dowson, and he gave it the most scrupulous care: each poem which made several appearances was overhauled before it was passed for press once more, and sometimes the whole punctuation scheme was altered.

[1] T. W. H. Crosland, *Op. cit.*
[2] See p. 287.

Frequently the tendency is to lighten the punctuation, to replace colons by semi-colons, semi-colons by commas, and to remove the latter altogether where they can be spared; but there are several outstanding exceptions and it would be dangerous to conclude that a gradual lightening of punctuation was the object of this careful attention. Rather it must be said again that however diffident Dowson may have appeared, he was deeply interested in his poetry and, when his health permitted, bestowed on it the endless hours that alone could bring such delicately tinted gems to their brilliant degree of polish. Though he may often have failed to improve on what he had already written, unlike some unfortunate men who cannot leave their work alone he never spoiled.

The most important feature in this edition must, obviously, be the incorporation of the new poems which appear on pages 137–188. With the exception of three, two of which are fragments, all these are taken from what was at one time called the Flower note-book. This volume was for some years one of the major ornaments of A. J. A. Symons' remarkable library of '90's books, unfortunately dispersed in 1933; thence it passed into the possession of Sir Newman Flower, my father. It is now in the Morgan Library, New York. The importance of this note-book will be realized from the fact that it yields no less than forty poems that had not previously been published, which is nine more than Dowson printed in *Decorations* and only three less than he included in *Verses*, his major volume. In addition, the note-book gave variant versions of twenty-seven poems already published, and thirty-six dates of composition. Nor must it be presumed that because Dowson had this note-book by him and did not choose to print many of the poems in it, that they were not worthy of appearance. It is not hard to see, for instance, that the *Sonnets to a Little Girl*, which to-day serve only to raise their author in our estimation as a master of the Sonnet, must have meant something personal to him which he was loath to bring before a sceptical public. Those who have declared that Dowson could do no more than write charming and regretful poetry will be surprised by the violence of the lines against Lady Burton, another poem which circumstances must have prevented from appearing.

The Flower note-book is an ordinary black-covered book, such as can be purchased in any stationer's to-day; the paper is of better quality than its modern counterpart, but its black leatherette covers and marbled endpapers are familiar to everyone. Dowson was obviously careful to write in it a fair copy of any poem with which he was at all satisfied, and to add, wherever he remembered it, the date of composition and any details of sales to periodicals. The Analysis in Appendix II (page 229) shows that, after an erratic start in 1886 or 1887, when a number of poems were probably copied into the then recently purchased book, the sequence is chronological. The book is full and a number of pages here and there have been torn out. In spite of his tragic and irregular life, there is evidence that Dowson was methodical, especially with regard to his work; presumably he went on to another note-book after this one was filled, and it may be that the few grey pages on which *De Amore* is written, that have been slipped loose into this one, formed part of it. The rest of it must have perished with his scanty belongings somewhere in Brittany towards the end of his life.

Every admirer of Dowson's poetry is familiar with the original appearance of *Verses*, with its white cover relieved only by the lovely Beardsley design. It must rank as one of the most representative and most charming pieces of 'nineties typography. When it appeared, Smithers had not been in business as a publisher long, though as a bookseller he had already been active for some time. Before his friendship with Smithers sprang up, Dowson had considered placing his poems with Elkin Mathews; in fact, Mathews regarded the matter as settled and spoke of the book as on his list. But in the end Dowson sent the MS. to Smithers, who probably made a better book than Mathews would have done.

Some years previously Plarr had suggested to Dowson that they should produce a joint volume of their poetry; *A Coronal*, which was used as the second poem in *Verses*, was to open the volume and give it its title. Lack of funds, however, killed the idea of a privately printed volume and the scheme was dropped; Dowson, we know, was keeping the Flower note-book up to date at that time, for, when Plarr wrote suggesting the volume, he replied that he would look in his "'Poesie Schublade' as represented by a small MSS. book" to see what he could find.[1] When the time came for him to assemble *Verses*, the note-book was full, and he took thirteen poems from it, among them *Cynara, Amore Umbratilis, Ad Domnulam Suam* and *Nuns of the Perpetual Adoration*.

Decorations has always been considered as an inferior volume to *Verses*, and the product of a failing genius. This is not altogether true: obviously Dowson's genius was by no means on the decline, since fourteen of the best poems in the book were written by 1892, at the same time as *Verses*, and it is not too much to presume that the rest followed very soon after in the next note-book. On the other hand, *Decorations* was certainly a second gathering from sources that had already yielded the previous volume. Again, the point of view which Dowson adopted in each book must be considered. *Verses*, expressing his sadness because the child of whom he was so fond was growing up, losing her simplicity and making life too complicated:

> *I watched the glory of her childhood change,*
> *Half-sorrowful to find the child I knew . . .*
> *Become a maid, mysterious and strange . . .*[2]

with a few poems added on the sadness of life in general, is autumn. *Decorations* is winter; the star, that before was falling and fading from its fiery heat is now no more than a stone lying dead and cold—parting has deepened into death. There are poems in *Decorations*, with its first title of *Love's Aftermath*, which would have been out of place in *Verses*, and a second choice is not necessarily second-rate. *Decorations*, after all, contains the four magnificent translations from

[1] Plarr, *Reminiscences of Ernest Dowson*, 1914.
[2] *Growth, Verses.*

Verlaine, *Carthusians, The Dead Child,* and the *Song* beginning
"All that a man may pray", and it was by no means an incon-
siderable offering to lay before his disparaging critics. What
its reception would have been we can never tell, for the
reviews, when they did appear, were tempered by reverence
for the dead and vague references to the author's unhappy
life. The Dowson legend had begun.

The Pierrot of the Minute, like the rest of Dowson's poetry,
was comparatively early work. It was written in a hurry
and performed in 1893, though it was not published until
three years later. Charming as it is, Dowson did not care
much for it, and Beardsley loathed it, muttering in letters to
his friends while he was doing the decorations. It is repre-
sentative of its period—Mr. Holbrook Jackson has pointed
out that white is the colour of the 'nineties, and the *Pierrot
of the Minute* is a symphony in white—but even though we
have Mr. Jackson's warning ringing in our ears, "there is
even now a risk of overestimating its (the 'nineties) achieve-
ment", I doubt whether it is any worse poetry than many
highly esteemed and equally "precious" products of the
Elizabethan age.

In *Verses, Decorations,* and *The Pierrot of the Minute* I have
followed the text of the first editions, 1896, 1899 and 1896
respectively, particular attention to the punctuation being
necessary, since in many instances it became corrupted later.
In the case of the unpublished poems, and often in the un-
collected poems, there is but one text. A great many of
Dowson's verses appeared in periodicals and the first and
second *Books of the Rhymers' Club,* and they were never passed
for press without stringent revision. Furthermore, he was
in the habit of sending copies of his poems in letters to friends
as soon as he had written them. It is not surprising, therefore,
that there are in many of the poems an alarming number
of variants, which have swollen the notes to large proportions.
Nuns of the Perpetual Adoration is an extreme example. This
poem was first printed in the *Century Guild Hobby Horse,*
then in the first *Book of the Rhymers' Club,* and finally in *Verses.*
There are in addition three MS. versions in the author's hand

extant, and Lionel Johnson's copy of the Rhymers' Club book containing corrections made by him with Dowson's authority. These sources, in a poem of thirty-two lines, yield seventy-two variants, including an alternative version of one stanza. Many of these are small questions of punctuation, and in some cases the alteration of a capital for a lower-case letter, or vice versa; but I have included them all without discrimination, since, in the first case, Dowson's punctuation is a subject that is full of interest, and in the second the presence or absence of capitals in a line can alter stress. While it has been necessary to load the notes with details that some may find tedious or unnecessary, I have endeavoured to make amends by a form of compression in the arrangement of them: minor variants have as far as possible been run on with the minimum of wasted space, while points that are significant, such as altered wording or punctuation that changes meaning or rhythm, have been allotted a line to themselves.

I have been deeply indebted to my late father, Sir Newman Flower, who by making the note-book available to me originally made a fresh edition of Dowson's poems desirable. I am also grateful to the memory of those who, over the years, allowed me to consult their autograph material: Arthur Moore, Canon John Gray, Michael Holland, J. Harlin O'Connell and Messrs. Elkin Mathews. Lastly I owe a particular debt to my old friend A. J. A. Symons who, from 1930 until his death in 1941, encouraged me with his advice, delighted me with his conversation and honoured me with his friendship.

Kensington, October 1934
Marylebone, 1949
Reigate, 1967

POSTSCRIPT

As the dateline of my Introduction shows, this edition of Dowson's poems was first published a number of years ago and revised just after the Second World War. No new verses have come to light since, and this edition is being reissued now in the year of the centenary of Dowson's birth.

Since 1949 I have discovered a great deal more about the details of Dowson's life. I am happy to say that everything fresh which I have learnt is to his credit and underlines the fact that he was more hardworking and more deeply appreciated by his friends than his detractors thought.

Although I have rehandled the Introduction in some details, I have not materially altered it because, for better or worse, it is as good as I am capable of making it.

For those who wish to know more about Dowson, the mass of new material which has come to light will be found set out in detail in *The Collected Letters of Ernest Dowson* edited by Mr. Henry Maas and myself which is about to appear.

D F

VERSES

Vitae summa brevis spem nos vetat incohare longam.

They are not long, the weeping and the laughter,
    Love and desire and hate:
I think they have no portion in us after
    We pass the gate.

They are not long, the days of wine and roses:
    Out of a misty dream
Our path emerges for a while, then closes
    Within a dream.

IN PREFACE: FOR ADELAIDE

TO you, who are my verses, as on some very future day, if you ever care to read them, you will understand, would it not be somewhat trivial to dedicate any one verse, as I may do, in all humility, to my friends? Trivial, too, perhaps, only to name you even here? Trivial, presumptuous? For I need not write your name for you at least to know that this and all my work is made for you in the first place, and I need not to be reminded by my critics that I have no silver tongue such as were fit to praise you. So for once you shall go indedicate, if not quite anonymous; and I will only commend my little book to you in sentences far beyond my poor compass which will help you perhaps to be kind to it:

"*Votre personne, vos moindres mouvements me semblaient avoir dans le monde une importance extra-humaine. Mon cœur comme de la poussière se soulevait derrière vos pas. Vous me faisiez l'effet d'un clair-de-lune par une nuit d'été, quand tout est parfums, ombres douces, blancheurs, infini; et les délices de la chair et de l'âme étaient contenues pour moi dans votre nom que je me répétais en tachant de le baiser sur mes lèvres.*

"*Quelquefois vos paroles me reviennent comme un écho lointain, comme le son d'une cloche apporté par le vent; et il me semble que vous êtes là quand je lis des passages de l'amour dans les livres. . . . Tout ce qu'on y blâme d'exagéré, vous me l'avez fait ressentir.*"

PONT-AVEN, FINISTÈRE, 1896.

A CORONAL

*With His songs and Her days to His Lady
and to Love*

Violets and leaves of vine,
　Into a frail, fair wreath
We gather and entwine:
　A wreath for Love to wear,
　Fragrant as his own breath,
To crown his brow divine,
　All day till night is near.
Violets and leaves of vine
We gather and entwine.

Violets and leaves of vine
　For Love that lives a day,
We gather and entwine.
　All day till Love is dead,
　Till eve falls, cold and gray,
These blossoms, yours and mine,
　Love wears upon his head.
Violets and leaves of vine
We gather and entwine.

Violets and leaves of vine,
   For Love when poor Love dies
We gather and entwine.
   This wreath that lives a day
   Over his pale, cold eyes,
Kissed shut by Proserpine,
   At set of sun we lay:
Violets and leaves of vine
We gather and entwine.

NUNS OF THE PERPETUAL ADORATION

For THE COUNTESS SOBIESKA VON PLATT

Calm, sad, secure; behind high convent walls,
  These watch the sacred lamp, these watch and pray:
And it is one with them when evening falls,
  And one with them the cold return of day.

These heed not time; their nights and days they make
  Into a long, returning rosary,
Whereon their lives are threaded for Christ's sake:
  Meekness and vigilance and chastity.

A vowed patrol, in silent companies,
  Life-long they keep before the living Christ:
In the dim church, their prayers and penances
  Are fragrant incense to the Sacrificed.

Outside, the world is wild and passionate;
  Man's weary laughter and his sick despair
Entreat at their impenetrable gate:
  They heed no voices in their dream of prayer.

They saw the glory of the world displayed;
  They saw the bitter of it, and the sweet;
They knew the roses of the world should fade,
  And be trod under by the hurrying feet.

Therefore they rather put away desire,
   And crossed their hands and came to sanctuary;
And veiled their heads and put on coarse attire:
   Because their comeliness was vanity.

And there they rest; they have serene insight
   Of the illuminating dawn to be:
Mary's sweet Star dispels for them the night,
   The proper darkness of humanity.

Calm, sad, secure; with faces worn and mild:
   Surely their choice of vigil is the best?
Yea! for our roses fade, the world is wild;
   But there, beside the altar, there, is rest.

VILLANELLE OF SUNSET

Come hither, Child! and rest:
This is the end of day,
Behold the weary West!

Sleep rounds with equal zest
Man's toil and children's play:
Come hither, Child! and rest.

My white bird, seek thy nest,
Thy drooping head down lay:
Behold the weary West!

Now are the flowers confest
Of slumber: sleep, as they!
Come hither, Child! and rest.

Now eve is manifest,
And homeward lies our way:
Behold the weary West!

Tired flower! upon my breast,
I would wear thee alway:
Come hither, Child! and rest;
Behold, the weary West!

MY LADY APRIL

For LÉOPOLD NELKEN

Dew on her robe and on her tangled hair;
Twin dewdrops for her eyes; behold her pass,
With dainty step brushing the young, green grass,
The while she trills some high, fantastic air,
Full of all feathered sweetness: she is fair,
And all her flower-like beauty, as a glass,
Mirrors out hope and love: and still, alas!
Traces of tears her languid lashes wear.
Say, doth she weep for very wantonness?
Or is it that she dimly doth foresee
Across her youth the joys grow less and less,
The burden of the days that are to be:
Autumn and withered leaves and vanity,
And winter bringing end in barrenness.

TO ONE IN BEDLAM

For HENRY DAVRAY

With delicate, mad hands, behind his sordid bars,
Surely he hath his posies, which they tear and twine;
Those scentless wisps of straw, that miserably line
His strait, caged universe, whereat the dull world stares,

Pedant and pitiful. O, how his rapt gaze wars
With their stupidity! Know they what dreams divine
Lift his long, laughing reveries like enchaunted wine,
And make his melancholy germane to the stars'?

O lamentable brother! if those pity thee,
Am I not fain of all thy lone eyes promise me;
Half a fool's kingdom, far from men who sow and reap,
All their days, vanity? Better than mortal flowers,
Thy moon-kissed roses seem: better than love or sleep,
The star-crowned solitude of thine oblivious hours!

AD DOMNULAM SUAM

Little lady of my heart!
  Just a little longer,
Love me: we will pass and part,
  Ere this love grow stronger.

I have loved thee, Child! too well,
  To do aught but leave thee:
Nay! my lips should never tell
  Any tale, to grieve thee.

Little lady of my heart!
  Just a little longer,
I may love thee: we will part,
  Ere my love grow stronger.

Soon thou leavest fairy-land;
  Darker grow thy tresses:
Soon no more of hand in hand;
  Soon no more caresses!

Little lady of my heart!
  Just a little longer,
Be a child: then, we will part,
  Ere this love grow stronger.

AMOR UMBRATILIS

A gift of Silence, sweet!
  Who may not ever hear:
To lay down at your unobservant feet,
  Is all the gift I bear.

I have no songs to sing,
  That you should heed or know:
I have no lilies, in full hands, to fling
  Across the path you go.

I cast my flowers away,
  Blossoms unmeet for you!
The garland I have gathered in my day:
  My rosemary and rue.

I watch you pass and pass,
  Serene and cold: I lay
My lips upon your trodden, daisied grass,
  And turn my life away.

Yea, for I cast you, sweet!
  This one gift, you shall take:
Like ointment, on your unobservant feet,
  My silence, for your sake.

AMOR PROFANUS

For GABRIEL DE LAUTREC

Beyond the pale of memory,
In some mysterious dusky grove;
A place of shadows utterly,
Where never coos the turtle-dove,
A world forgotten of the sun:
I dreamed we met when day was done,
And marvelled at our ancient love.

Met there by chance, long kept apart,
We wandered, through the darkling glades;
And that old language of the heart
We sought to speak: alas! poor shades!
Over our pallid lips had run
The waters of oblivion,
Which crown all loves of men or maids.

In vain we stammered: from afar
Our old desire shone cold and dead:
That time was distant as a star,
When eyes were bright and lips were red.
And still we went with downcast eye
And no delight in being nigh,
Poor shadows most uncomforted.

Ah, Lalage! while life is ours,
Hoard not thy beauty rose and white,
But pluck the pretty, fleeting flowers
That deck our little path of light:
For all too soon we twain shall tread
The bitter pastures of the dead:
Estranged, sad spectres of the night.

VILLANELLE OF MARGUERITES

For MISS EUGÉNIE MAGNUS

"*A little, passionately, not at all?*"
She casts the snowy petals on the air:
And what care we how many petals fall!

Nay, wherefore seek the seasons to forestall?
It is but playing, and she will not care,
A little, passionately, not at all!

She would not answer us if we should call
Across the years: her visions are too fair;
And what care we how many petals fall!

She knows us not, nor recks if she enthrall
With voice and eyes and fashion of her hair,
A little, passionately, not at all!

Knee-deep she goes in meadow grasses tall,
Kissed by the daisies that her fingers tear:
And what care we how many petals fall!

We pass and go: but she shall not recall
What men we were, nor all she made us bear:
"*A little, passionately, not at all!*"
And what care we how many petals fall!

YVONNE OF BRITTANY

For MARMADUKE LANGDALE

In your mother's apple-orchard,
  Just a year ago, last spring:
Do you remember, Yvonne!
  The dear trees lavishing
Rain of their starry blossoms
  To make you a coronet?
Do you ever remember, Yvonne?
  As I remember yet.

In your mother's apple-orchard,
  When the world was left behind:
You were shy, so shy, Yvonne!
  But your eyes were calm and kind.
We spoke of the apple harvest,
  When the cider press is set,
And such-like trifles, Yvonne!
  That doubtless you forget.

In the still, soft Breton twilight,
  We were silent; words were few,
Till your mother came out chiding,
  For the grass was bright with dew:
But I know your heart was beating,
  Like a fluttered, frightened dove.
Do you ever remember, Yvonne?
  That first faint flush of love?

In the fulness of midsummer,
  When the apple-bloom was shed,
Oh, brave was your surrender,
  Though shy the words you said.
I was glad, so glad, Yvonne!
  To have led you home at last;
Do you ever remember, Yvonne!
  How swiftly the days passed?

In your mother's apple-orchard
  It is grown too dark to stray,
There is none to chide you, Yvonne!
  You are over far away.
There is dew on your grave grass, Yvonne!
  But your feet it shall not wet:
No, you never remember, Yvonne!
  And I shall soon forget.

BENEDICTIO DOMINI

For SELWYN IMAGE

Without, the sullen noises of the street!
  The voice of London, inarticulate,
Hoarse and blaspheming, surges in to meet
  The silent blessing of the Immaculate.

Dark is the church, and dim the worshippers,
  Hushed with bowed heads as though by some old spell,
While through the incense-laden air there stirs
  The admonition of a silver bell.

Dark is the church, save where the altar stands,
  Dressed like a bride, illustrious with light,
Where one old priest exalts with tremulous hands
  The one true solace of man's fallen plight.

Strange silence here: without, the sounding street
  Heralds the world's swift passage to the fire:
O Benediction, perfect and complete!
  When shall men cease to suffer and desire?

GROWTH

I watched the glory of her childhood change,
Half-sorrowful to find the child I knew,
   (Loved long ago in lily-time)
Become a maid, mysterious and strange,
With fair, pure eyes—dear eyes, but not the eyes I knew
    Of old, in the olden time !

Till on my doubting soul the ancient good
Of her dear childhood in the new disguise
   Dawned, and I hastened to adore
The glory of her waking maidenhood,
And found the old tenderness within her deepening eyes,
    But kinder than before.

AD MANUS PUELLAE

For LEONARD SMITHERS

I was always a lover of ladies' hands!
  Or ever mine heart came here to tryst,
For the sake of your carved white hands' commands;
  The tapering fingers, the dainty wrist;
  The hands of a girl were what I kissed.

I remember an hand like a *fleur-de-lys*
  When it slid from its silken sheath, her glove;
With its odours passing ambergris:
  And that was the empty husk of a love.
  Oh, how shall I kiss your hands enough?

They are pale with the pallor of ivories;
  But they blush to the tips like a curled sea-shell:
What treasure, in kingly treasuries,
  Of gold, and spice for the thurible,
  Is sweet as her hands to hoard and tell?

I know not the way from your finger-tips,
  Nor how I shall gain the higher lands,
The citadel of your sacred lips:
  I am captive still of my pleasant bands,
  The hands of a girl, and most your hands.

FLOS LUNAE

For YVANHOÉ RAMBOSSON

I would not alter thy cold eyes,
Nor trouble the calm fount of speech
With aught of passion or surprise.
The heart of thee I cannot reach:
I would not alter thy cold eyes!

I would not alter thy cold eyes;
Nor have thee smile, nor make thee weep:
Though all my life droops down and dies,
Desiring thee, desiring sleep,
I would not alter thy cold eyes.

I would not alter thy cold eyes;
I would not change thee if I might,
To whom my prayers for incense rise,
Daughter of dreams! my moon of night!
I would not alter thy cold eyes.

I would not alter thy cold eyes,
With trouble of the human heart:
Within their glance my spirit lies,
A frozen thing, alone, apart;
I would not alter thy cold eyes.

NON SUM QUALIS ERAM BONAE
SUB REGNO CYNARAE

Last night, ah, yesternight, betwixt her lips and mine
There fell thy shadow, Cynara! thy breath was shed
Upon my soul between the kisses and the wine;
And I was desolate and sick of an old passion,
    Yea, I was desolate and bowed my head:
I have been faithful to thee, Cynara! in my fashion.

All night upon mine heart I felt her warm heart beat,
Night-long within mine arms in love and sleep she lay;
Surely the kisses of her bought red mouth were sweet;
But I was desolate and sick of an old passion,
    When I awoke and found the dawn was gray:
I have been faithful to thee, Cynara! in my fashion.

I have forgot much, Cynara! gone with the wind,
Flung roses, roses riotously with the throng,
Dancing, to put thy pale, lost lilies out of mind;
But I was desolate and sick of an old passion,
    Yea, all the time, because the dance was long:
I have been faithful to thee, Cynara! in my fashion.

I cried for madder music and for stronger wine,
But when the feast is finished and the lamps expire,
Then falls thy shadow, Cynara! the night is thine;
And I am desolate and sick of an old passion,
    Yea hungry for the lips of my desire:
I have been faithful to thee, Cynara! in my fashion.

VANITAS

For VINCENT O'SULLIVAN

Beyond the need of weeping,
   Beyond the reach of hands,
May she be quietly sleeping,
   In what dim nebulous lands?
Ah, she who understands!

The long, long winter weather,
   These many years and days,
Since she, and Death, together,
   Left me the wearier ways:
And now, these tardy bays!

The crown and victor's token:
   How are they worth to-day?
The one word left unspoken,
   It were late now to say:
But cast the palm away!

For once, ah once, to meet her,
   Drop laurel from tired hands:
Her cypress were the sweeter,
   In her oblivious lands:
Haply she understands!

Yet, crossed that weary river,
   In some ulterior land,
Or anywhere, or ever,
   Will she stretch out a hand?
And will she understand?

EXILE

For CONAL HOLMES O'CONNELL O'RIORDAN

By the sad waters of separation
  Where we have wandered by divers ways,
I have but the shadow and imitation
  Of the old memorial days.

In music I have no consolation,
  No roses are pale enough for me;
The sound of the waters of separation
  Surpasseth roses and melody.

By the sad waters of separation
  Dimly I hear from an hidden place
The sigh of mine ancient adoration:
  Hardly can I remember your face.

If you be dead, no proclamation
  Sprang to me over the waste, gray sea:
Living, the waters of separation
  Sever for ever your soul from me.

No man knoweth our desolation;
  Memory pales of the old delight;
While the sad waters of separation
  Bear us on to the ultimate night.

SPLEEN

For ARTHUR SYMONS

I was not sorrowful, I could not weep,
And all my memories were put to sleep.

I watched the river grow more white **and strange,**
All day till evening I watched it change.

All day till evening I watched the rain
Beat wearily upon the window pane.

I was not sorrowful, but only tired
Of everything that ever I desired.

Her lips, her eyes, all day became to me
The shadow of a shadow utterly.

All day mine hunger for her heart became
Oblivion, until the evening came,

And left me sorrowful, inclined to weep,
With all my memories that could not sleep.

O MORS! QUAM AMARA EST MEMORIA TUA HOMINI PACEM HABENTI IN SUBSTANTIIS SUIS

Exceeding sorrow
    Consumeth my sad heart!
Because to-morrow
    We must depart,
Now is exceeding sorrow
    All my part!

Give over playing,
    Cast thy viol away:
Merely laying
    Thine head my way:
Prithee, give over playing,
    Grave or gay.

Be no word spoken;
    Weep nothing: let a pale
Silence, unbroken
    Silence prevail!
Prithee, be no word spoken,
    Lest I fail!

Forget to-morrow!
   Weep nothing: only lay
In silent sorrow
   Thine head my way:
Let us forget to-morrow,
   This one day!

Ah, dans ces mornes séjours
Les jamais sont les toujours.
                PAUL VERLAINE

You would have understood me, had you waited;
    I could have loved you, dear! as well as he:
Had we not been impatient, dear! and fated
        Always to disagree.

What is the use of speech?   Silence were fitter:
    Lest we should still be wishing things unsaid.
Though all the words we ever spake were bitter,
        Shall I reproach you dead?

Nay, let this earth, your portion, likewise cover
    All the old anger, setting us apart:
Always, in all, in truth was I your lover;
        Always, I held your heart.

I have met other women who were tender,
    As you were cold, dear! with a grace as rare.
Think you, I turned to them, or made surrender,
        I who had found you fair?

Had we been patient, dear! ah, had you waited,
    I had fought death for you, better than he:
But from the very first, dear! we were fated
        Always to disagree.

Late, late, I come to you, now death discloses
Love that in life was not to be our part:
On your low lying mound between the roses,
　　Sadly I cast my heart.

I would not waken you: nay! this is fitter;
　　Death and the darkness give you unto me;
Here we who loved so, were so cold and bitter,
　　Hardly can disagree.

APRIL LOVE

For ARTHUR CECIL HILLIER

We have walked in Love's land a little way,
　We have learnt his lesson a little while,
And shall we not part at the end of day,
　　With a sigh, a smile?

A little while in the shine of the sun,
　We were twined together, joined lips, forgot
How the shadows fall when the day is done,
　　And when Love is not.

We have made no vows—there will none be broke,
　Our love was free as the wind on the hill,
There was no word said we need wish unspoke,
　　We have wrought no ill.

So shall we not part at the end of day,
　Who have loved and lingered a little while,
Join lips for the last time, go our way,
　　With a sigh, a smile?

VAIN HOPE

Sometimes, to solace my sad heart, I say,
 Though late it be, though lily-time be past,
 Though all the summer skies be overcast,
Haply I will go down to her, some day,
 And cast my rests of life before her feet,
That she may have her will of me, being so sweet,
 And none gainsay!

So might she look on me with pitying eyes,
 And lay calm hands of healing on my head:
 "Because of thy long pains be comforted;
For I, even I, am Love: sad soul, arise!"
 So, for her graciousness, I might at last
Gaze on the very face of Love, and hold Him fast
 In no disguise.

Haply, I said, she will take pity on me,
 Though late I come, long after lily-time,
 With burden of waste days and drifted rhyme:
Her kind, calm eyes, down drooping maidenly,
 Shall change, grow soft: there yet is time, meseems,
I said, for solace; though I know these things are dreams
 And may not be!

VAIN RESOLVES

I said: "There is an end of my desire:
  Now have I sown, and I have harvested,
And these are ashes of an ancient fire,
  Which, verily, shall not be quickened.
Now will I take me to a place of peace,
    Forget mine heart's desire;
In solitude and prayer, work out my soul's release.

"I shall forget her eyes, how cold they were;
  Forget her voice, how soft it was and low,
With all my singing that she did not hear,
  And all my service that she did not know.
I shall not hold the merest memory
    Of any days that were,
Within those solitudes where I will fasten me."

And once she passed, and once she raised her eyes,
  And smiled for courtesy, and nothing said:
And suddenly the old flame did uprise,
  And all my dead desire was quickened.
Yea! as it hath been, it shall ever be,
    Most passionless, pure eyes!
Which never shall grow soft, nor change, nor pity me.

A REQUIEM

For JOHN GRAY

Neobule, being tired,
Far too tired to laugh or weep,
From the hours, rosy and gray,
Hid her golden face away.
Neobule, fain of sleep,
Slept at last as she desired!

Neobule! is it well,
That you haunt the hollow lands,
Where the poor, dead people stray,
Ghostly, pitiful and gray,
Plucking, with their spectral hands,
Scentless blooms of asphodel?

Neobule, tired to death
Of the flowers that I threw
On her flower-like, fair feet,
Sighed for blossoms not so sweet,
Lunar roses pale and blue,
Lilies of the world beneath.

Neobule! ah, too tired
Of the dreams and days above!
Where the poor, dead people stray,
Ghostly, pitiful and gray,
Out of life and out of love,
Sleeps the sleep which she desired.

BEATA SOLITUDO

For SAM. SMITH

What land of Silence,
   Where pale stars shine
On apple-blossom
   And dew-drenched vine,
   Is yours and mine?

The silent valley
   That we will find,
Where all the voices
   Of humankind
   Are left behind.

There all forgetting,
   Forgotten quite,
We will repose us,
   With our delight
   Hid out of sight.

The world forsaken,
   And out of mind
Honour and labour,
   We shall not find
   The stars unkind.

And men shall travail,
  And laugh and weep;
But we have vistas
  Of gods asleep,
  With dreams as deep.

A land of Silence,
  Where pale stars shine
On apple-blossoms
  And dew-drenched vine,
  Be yours and mine!

TERRE PROMISE

For HERBERT P. HORNE

Even now the fragrant darkness of her hair
Had brushed my cheek; and once, in passing by,
Her hand upon my hand lay tranquilly:
What things unspoken trembled in the air!

Always I know, how little severs me
From mine heart's country, that is yet so far;
And must I lean and long across a bar,
That half a word would shatter utterly?

Ah might it be, that just by touch of hand,
Or speaking silence, shall the barrier fall;
And she shall pass, with no vain words at all,
But droop into mine arms, and understand!

AUTUMNAL

For ALEXANDER TEIXEIRA DE MATTOS

Pale amber sunlight falls across
   The reddening October trees,
   That hardly sway before a breeze
As soft as summer: summer's loss
   Seems little, dear! on days like these!

Let misty autumn be our part!
   The twilight of the year is sweet:
   Where shadow and the darkness meet
Our love, a twilight of the heart
   Eludes a little time's deceit.

Are we not better and at home
   In dreamful Autumn, we who deem
   No harvest joy is worth a dream?
A little while and night shall come,
   A little while, then, let us dream.

Beyond the pearled horizons lie
   Winter and night: awaiting these
   We garner this poor hour of ease,
Until love turn from us and die
   Beneath the drear November trees.

IN TEMPORE SENECTUTIS

When I am old,
   And sadly steal apart,
Into the dark and cold,
   Friend of my heart!
Remember, if you can,
Not him who lingers, but that other man,
Who loved and sang, and had a beating heart,—
   When I am old!

When I am old,
   And all Love's ancient fire
Be tremulous and cold:
   My soul's desire!
Remember, if you may,
Nothing of you and me but yesterday,
When heart on heart we bid the years conspire
   To make us old.

When I am old,
   And every star above
Be pitiless and cold:
   My life's one love!
Forbid me not to go:
Remember nought of us but long ago,
And not at last, how love and pity strove
   When I grew old!

VILLANELLE OF HIS LADY'S TREASURES

I took her dainty eyes, as well
  As silken tendrils of her hair:
And so I made a Villanelle!

I took her voice, a silver bell,
  As clear as song, as soft as prayer;
I took her dainty eyes as well.

It may be, said I, who can tell,
  These things shall be my less despair?
And so I made a Villanelle!

I took her whiteness virginal
  And from her cheek two roses rare:
I took her dainty eyes as well.

I said: "It may be possible
  Her image from my heart to tear!"
And so I made a Villanelle.

I stole her laugh, most musical:
  I wrought it in with artful care;
I took her dainty eyes as well;
And so I made a Villanelle.

GRAY NIGHTS

For CHARLES SAYLE

Awhile we wandered (thus it is I dream!)
Through a long, sandy track of No Man's Land,
Where only poppies grew among the sand,
The which we, plucking, cast with scant esteem,
And ever sadlier, into the sad stream,
Which followed us, as we went, hand in hand,
Under the estrangèd stars, a road unplanned,
Seeing all things in the shadow of a dream.
And ever sadlier, as the stars expired,
We found the poppies rarer, till thine eyes
Grown all my light, to light me were too tired,
And at their darkening, that no surmise
Might haunt me of the lost days we desired,
After them all I flung those memories!

VESPERAL

For HUBERT CRACKANTHORPE

Strange grows the river on the sunless evenings!
The river comforts me, grown spectral, vague and dumb:
Long was the day; at last the consoling shadows come:
Sufficient for the day are the day's evil things!

Labour and longing and despair the long day brings;
Patient till evening men watch the sun go west;
Deferred, expected night at last brings sleep and rest:
Sufficient for the day are the day's evil things!

At last the tranquil Angelus of evening rings
Night's curtain down for comfort and oblivion
Of all the vanities observèd by the sun:
Sufficient for the day are the day's evil things!

So, some time, when the last of all our evenings
Crowneth memorially the last of all our days,
Not loth to take his poppies man goes down and says,
"Sufficient for the day were the day's evil things!"

THE GARDEN OF SHADOW

Love heeds no more the sighing of the wind
Against the perfect flowers: thy garden's close
Is grown a wilderness, where none shall find
One strayed, last petal of one last year's rose.

O bright, bright hair!   O mouth like a ripe fruit!
Can famine be so nigh to harvesting?
Love, that was songful, with a broken lute
In grass of graveyards goeth murmuring.

Let the wind blow against the perfect flowers,
And all thy garden change and glow with spring:
Love is grown blind with no more count of hours,
Nor part in seed-time nor in harvesting.

SOLI CANTARE PERITI ARCADES

For AUBREY BEARDSLEY

Oh, I would live in a dairy,
  And its Colin I would be,
And many a rustic fairy
  Should churn the milk with me.

Or the fields should be my pleasure,
  And my flocks should follow me,
Piping a frolic measure
  For Joan or Marjorie.

For the town is black and weary,
  And I hate the London street;
But the country ways are cheery,
  And country lanes are sweet.

Good luck to you, Paris ladies!
  Ye are over fine and nice,
I know where the country maid is,
  Who needs not asking twice.

Ye are brave in your silks and satins,
  As ye mince about the Town;
But her feet go free in pattens,
  If she wear a russet gown.

If she be not queen nor goddess
  She shall milk my brown-eyed herds,
And the breasts beneath her boddice
  Are whiter than her curds.

So I will live in a dairy,
  And its Colin I will be,
And it's Joan that I will marry,
  Or, haply, Marjorie.

ON THE BIRTH OF A
FRIEND'S CHILD

For VICTOR AND NELLIE PLARR

Mark the day white, on which the Fates have smiled:
Eugenio and Egeria have a child.
On whom abundant grace kind Jove imparts
If she but copy either parent's parts.
Then, Muses! long devoted to her race,
Grant her Egeria's virtues and her face;
Nor stop your bounty there, but add to it
Eugenio's learning and Eugenio's wit.

EXTREME UNCTION

For LIONEL JOHNSON

Upon the eyes, the lips, the feet,
  On all the passages of sense,
The atoning oil is spread with sweet
  Renewal of lost innocence.

The feet, that lately ran so fast
  To meet desire, are soothly sealed;
The eyes, that were so often cast
  On vanity, are touched and healed.

From troublous sights and sounds set free;
  In such a twilight hour of breath,
Shall one retrace his life, or see,
  Through shadows, the true face of death?

Vials of mercy! Sacring oils!
  I know not where nor when I come,
Nor through what wanderings and toils,
  To crave of you Viaticum.

Yet, when the walls of flesh grow weak,
  In such an hour, it well may be,
Through mist and darkness, light will break,
  And each anointed sense will see.

AMANTIUM IRAE

When this, our rose, is faded,
　And these, our days, are done,
In lands profoundly shaded
　From tempest and from sun:
Ah, once more come together,
　Shall we forgive the past,
And safe from worldly weather
　Possess our souls at last?

Or in our place of shadows
　Shall still we stretch an hand
To green, remembered meadows,
　Of that old pleasant land?
And vainly there foregathered,
　Shall we regret the sun?
The rose of love, ungathered?
　The bay, we have not won?

Ah, child! the world's dark marges
　May lead to Nevermore,
The stately funeral barges
　Sail for an unknown shore,
And love we vow to-morrow,
　And pride we serve to-day:
What if they both should borrow
　Sad hues of yesterday?

Our pride!   Ah, should we miss it,
  Or will it serve at last?
Our anger, if we kiss it,
  Is like a sorrow past.
While roses deck the garden,
  While yet the sun is high,
Doff sorry pride for pardon,
  Or ever love go by.

IMPENITENTIA ULTIMA

For ROBERT HARBOROUGH SHERARD

Before my light goes out for ever if God should give
    me a choice of graces,
    I would not reck of length of days, nor crave for
        things to be;
But cry: "One day of the great lost days, one face of
    all the faces,
    Grant me to see and touch once more and nothing
        more to see.

"For, Lord, I was free of all Thy flowers, but I chose
    the world's sad roses,
    And that is why my feet are torn and mine eyes are
        blind with sweat,
But at Thy terrible judgement-seat, when this my
    tired life closes,
    I am ready to reap whereof I sowed, and pay my
        righteous debt.

"But once before the sand is run and the silver thread
    is broken,
    Give me a grace and cast aside the veil of dolorous
        years,
Grant me one hour of all mine hours, and let me see
    for a token
    Her pure and pitiful eyes shine out, and bathe her
        feet with tears."

Her pitiful hands should calm, and her hair stream
    down and blind me,
  Out of the sight of night, and out of the reach of
    fear,
And her eyes should be my light whilst the sun went
    out behind me,
  And the viols in her voice be the last sound in mine
    ear.

Before the ruining waters fall and my life be carried
    under,
  And Thine anger cleave me through as a child cuts
    down a flower,
I will praise Thee, Lord, in Hell, while my limbs are
    racked asunder,
For the last sad sight of her face and the little grace
    of an hour.

A VALEDICTION

If we must part,
   Then let it be like this;
Not heart on heart,
   Nor with the useless anguish of a kiss;
But touch mine hand and say;
"*Until to-morrow or some other day,*
   If we must part."

Words are so weak
   When love hath been so strong:
Let silence speak:
   "*Life is a little while, and love is long;*
A time to sow and reap,
And after harvest a long time to sleep,
   But words are weak."

SAPIENTIA LUNAE

For ANDRÉ LEBEY

The wisdom of the world said unto me:
  "*Go forth and run, the race is to the brave;*
Perchance some honour tarrieth for thee!"
  "As tarrieth," I said, "for sure, the grave."
    For I had pondered on a rune of roses,
    Which to her votaries the moon discloses.

The wisdom of the world said: "*There are bays:*
  Go forth and run, for victory is good,
After the stress of the laborious days."
  "Yet," said I, "shall I be the worms' sweet food,"
    As I went musing on a rune of roses,
    Which in her hour, the pale, soft moon discloses.

Then said my voices: "*Wherefore strive or run,*
  On dusty highways ever, a vain race?
The long night cometh, starless, void of sun,
  What light shall serve thee like her golden face?"
    For I had pondered on a rune of roses,
    And knew some secrets which the moon discloses.

"Yea," said I, "for her eyes are pure and sweet
  As lilies, and the fragrance of her hair
Is many laurels; and it is not meet
  To run for shadows when the prize is here;"
    And I went reading in that rune of roses
    Which to her votaries the moon discloses.

Dum nos fata sinunt, oculos satiemus Amore.
PROPERTIUS

Cease smiling, Dear! a little while be sad,
　　Here in the silence, under the wan moon;
Sweet are thine eyes, but how can I be glad,
　　Knowing they change so soon?

For Love's sake, Dear, be silent!　Cover me
　　In the deep darkness of thy falling hair:
Fear is upon me and the memory
　　Of what is all men's share.

O could this moment be perpetuate!
　　Must we grow old, and leaden-eyed and gray,
And taste no more the wild and passionate
　　Love sorrows of to-day?

Grown old, and faded, Sweet! and past desire,
　　Let memory die, lest there be too much ruth,
Remembering the old, extinguished fire
　　Of our divine, lost youth.

O red pomegranate of thy perfect mouth!
　　My lips' life-fruitage, might I taste and die,
Here in thy garden, where the scented south
　　Wind chastens agony;

Reap death from thy live lips in one long kiss,
　And look my last into thine eyes and rest:
What sweets had life to me sweeter than this
　　Swift dying on thy breast?

Or, if that may not be, for Love's sake, Dear!
　Keep silence still, and dream that we shall lie,
Red mouth to mouth, entwined, and always hear
　　The south wind's melody,

Here in thy garden, through the sighing boughs,
　Beyond the reach of time and chance and change,
And bitter life and death, and broken vows,
　　That sadden and estrange.

SERAPHITA

Come not before me now, O visionary face!
Me tempest-tost, and borne along life's passionate sea;
Troublous and dark and stormy though my passage be;
Not here and now may we commingle or embrace,
Lest the loud anguish of the waters should efface
The bright illumination of thy memory,
Which dominates the night: rest, far away from me,
In the serenity of thine abiding-place!

But when the storm is highest, and the thunders blare,
And sea and sky are riven, O moon of all my night!
Stoop down but once in pity of my great despair,
And let thine hand, though over late to help, alight
But once upon my pale eyes and my drowning hair,
Before the great waves conquer in the last vain fight.

EPIGRAM

Because I am idolatrous and have besought,
With grievous supplication and consuming prayer,
The admirable image that my dreams have wrought
Out of her swan's neck and her dark, abundant hair:
The jealous gods, who brook no worship save their own,
Turned my live idol marble and her heart to stone.

QUID NON SPEREMUS, AMANTES?

For ARTHUR MOORE

Why is there in the least touch of her hands
  More grace than other women's lips bestow,
If love is but a slave in fleshly bands
  Of flesh to flesh, wherever love may go?

Why choose vain grief and heavy-hearted hours
  For her lost voice, and dear remembered hair,
If love may cull his honey from all flowers,
  And girls grow thick as violets, everywhere?

Nay! She is gone, and all things fall apart;
  Or she is cold, and vainly have we prayed;
And broken is the summer's splendid heart,
  And hope within a deep, dark grave is laid.

As man aspires and falls, yet a soul springs
  Out of his agony of flesh at last,
So love that flesh enthralls, shall rise on wings
  Soul-centred, when the rule of flesh is past.

Then, most High Love, or wreathed with myrtle sprays,
  Or crownless and forlorn, nor less a star,
Thee may I serve and follow, all my days,
  Whose thorns are sweet as never roses are!

CHANSON SANS PAROLES

In the deep violet air,
  Not a leaf is stirred;
  There is no sound heard,
But afar, the rare
  Trilled voice of a bird.

Is the wood's dim heart,
  And the fragrant pine,
  Incense, and a shrine
Of her coming?   Apart,
  I wait for a sign.

What the sudden hush said,
  She will hear, and forsake,
  Swift, for my sake,
Her green, grassy bed:
  She will hear and awake!

She will hearken and glide,
  From her place of deep rest,
  Dove-eyed, with the breast
Of a dove, to my side:
  The pines bow their crest.

I wait for a sign:
   The leaves to be waved,
   The tall tree-tops laved
In a flood of sunshine,
   This world to be saved!

In the deep violet air,
   Not a leaf is stirred;
   There is no sound heard,
But afar, the rare
   Trilled voice of a bird.

DECORATIONS

BEYOND

Love's aftermath! I think the time is now
That we must gather in, alone, apart
The saddest crop of all the crops that grow,
    Love's aftermath.
Ah, sweet,—sweet yesterday, the tears that start
Can not put back the dial; this is, I trow,
Our harvesting! Thy kisses chill my heart,
Our lips are cold; averted eyes avow
The twilight of poor love: we can but part,
Dumbly and sadly, reaping as we sow,
    Love's aftermath.

IN VERSE

DE AMORE

Shall one be sorrowful because of love,
  Which hath no earthly crown,
  Which lives and dies, unknown?
Because no words of his shall ever move
  Her maiden heart to own
  Him lord and destined master of her own:
Is Love so weak a thing as this,
  Who can not lie awake,
  Solely for his own sake,
For lack of the dear hands to hold, the lips to kiss,
  A mere heart-ache?

Nay, though love's victories be great and sweet,
  Nor vain and foolish toys,
  His crowned, earthly joys,
Is there no comfort then in love's defeat?
  Because he shall defer,
  For some short span of years all part in her,
  Submitting to forego
  The certain peace which happier lovers know;
Because he shall be utterly disowned,
  Nor length of service bring
  Her least awakening:
Foiled, frustrate and alone, misunderstood, discrowned,
      Is Love less King?

Grows not the world to him a fairer place,
  How far soever his days
  Pass from his lady's ways,
From mere encounter with her golden face?
  Though all his sighing be vain,
  Shall he be heavy-hearted and complain?
Is she not still a star,
Deeply to be desired, worshipped afar,
  A beacon-light to aid
  From bitter-sweet delights, Love's masquerade?
Though he lose many things,
  Though much he miss:
The heart upon his heart, the hand that clings,
  The memorable first kiss;
Love that is love at all,
Needs not an earthly coronal;
Love is himself his own exceeding great reward,
    A mighty lord!

Lord over life and all the ways of breath,
  Mighty and strong to save
  From the devouring grave;
Yea, whose dominion doth out-tyrant death,
  Thou who art life and death in one,
  The night, the sun;
Who art, when all things seem:
  Foiled, frustrate and forlorn, rejected of to-day,
  Go with me all my way,
And let me not blaspheme.

THE DEAD CHILD

Sleep on, dear, now
  The last sleep and the best,
And on thy brow,
  And on thy quiet breast,
Violets I throw.

Thy scanty years
  Were mine a little while;
Life had no fears
  To trouble thy brief smile
With toil or tears.

Lie still, and be
  For evermore a child!
Not grudgingly,
  Whom life has not defiled,
I render thee.

Slumber so deep,
  No man would rashly wake;
I hardly weep,
  Fain only, for thy sake,
To share thy sleep.

Yes, to be dead,
   Dead, here with thee to-day,—
When all is said
   'Twere good by thee to lay
My weary head.

The very best!
   Ah, child so tired of play,
I stand confessed:
   I want to come thy way,
And share thy rest.

CARTHUSIANS

Through what long heaviness, assayed in what strange fire,
  Have these white monks been brought into the way
    of peace,
Despising the world's wisdom and the world's desire,
  Which from the body of this death bring no release?

Within their austere walls no voices penetrate;
  A sacred silence only, as of death, obtains;
Nothing finds entry here of loud or passionate;
  This quiet is the exceeding profit of their pains.

From many lands they came, in divers fiery ways;
  Each knew at last the vanity of earthly joys;
And one was crowned with thorns, and one was crowned
    with bays,
  And each was tired at last of the world's foolish noise.

It was not theirs with Dominic to preach God's holy wrath,
  They were too stern to hear sweet Francis' gentle sway;
Theirs was a higher calling and a steeper path,
  To dwell alone with Christ, to meditate and pray.

A cloistered company, they are companionless,
  None knoweth here the secret of his brother's heart:
They are but come together for more loneliness,
  Whose bond is solitude and silence all their part.

O beatific life! Who is there shall gainsay,
 Your great refusal's victory, your little loss,
Deserting vanity for the more perfect way,
 The sweeter service of the most dolorous Cross.

Ye shall prevail at last! Surely ye shall prevail!
 Your silence and austerity shall win at last:
Desire and mirth, the world's ephemeral lights shall fail,
 The sweet star of your queen is never overcast.

We fling up flowers and laugh, we laugh across the wine;
 With wine we dull our souls and careful strains of art;
Our cups are polished skulls round which the roses twine:
 None dares to look at Death who leers and lurks apart.

Move on, white company, whom that has not sufficed!
 Our viols cease, our wine is death, our roses fail:
Pray for our heedlessness, O dwellers with the Christ!
 Though the world fall apart, surely ye shall prevail.

THE THREE WITCHES

All the moon-shed nights are over,
  And the days of gray and dun;
There is neither may nor clover,
  And the day and night are one.

Not an hamlet, not a city
  Meets our strained and tearless eyes;
In the plain without a pity,
  Where the wan grass droops and dies.

We shall wander through the meaning
  Of a day and see no light,
For our lichened arms are leaning
  On the ends of endless night.

We, the children of Astarte,
  Dear abortions of the moon,
In a gay and silent party,
  We are riding to you soon.

Burning ramparts, ever burning!
  To the flame which never dies
We are yearning, yearning, yearning,
  With our gay and tearless eyes.

In the plain without a pity,
  (Not an hamlet, not a city)
  Where the wan grass droops and dies.

VILLANELLE OF THE POET'S ROAD

Wine and woman and song,
  Three things garnish our way:
Yet is day over long.

Lest we do our youth wrong,
  Gather them while we may:
Wine and woman and song.

Three things render us strong,
  Vine leaves, kisses and bay;
Yet is day over long.

Unto us they belong,
  Us the bitter and gay,
Wine and woman and song.

We, as we pass along,
  Are sad that they will not stay;
Yet is day over long.

Fruits and flowers among,
  What is better than they:
Wine and woman and song?
  Yet is day over long.

VILLANELLE OF ACHERON

By the pale marge of Acheron,
  Methinks we shall pass restfully,
Beyond the scope of any sun.

There all men hie them one by one,
  Far from the stress of earth and sea,
By the pale marge of Acheron.

'Tis well when life and love is done,
  'Tis very well at last to be,
Beyond the scope of any sun.

No busy voices there shall stun
  Our ears: the stream flows silently
By the pale marge of Acheron.

There is the crown of labour won,
  The sleep of immortality,
Beyond the scope of any sun.

Life, of thy gifts I will have none,
  My queen is that Persephone,
By the pale marge of Acheron,
  Beyond the scope of any sun.

SAINT GERMAIN-EN-LAYE
(1887-95)

Through the green boughs I hardly saw thy face,
They twined so close: the sun was in mine eyes;
And now the sullen trees in sombre lace
Stand bare beneath the sinister, sad skies.

O sun and summer! Say in what far night,
The gold and green, the glory of thine head,
Of bough and branch have fallen? Oh, the white
Gaunt ghosts that flutter where thy feet have sped,

Across the terrace that is desolate,
And rang then with thy laughter, ghost of thee,
That holds its shroud up with most delicate,
Dead fingers, and behind the ghost of me,

Tripping fantastic with a mouth that jeers
At roseal flowers of youth the turbid streams
Toss in derision down the barren years
To death the host of all our golden dreams.

AFTER PAUL VERLAINE

I

Il pleut doucement sur la ville.

RIMBAUD

Tears fall within mine heart,
As rain upon the town:
Whence does this languor start,
Possessing all mine heart?

O sweet fall of the rain
Upon the earth and roofs!
Unto an heart in pain,
O music of the rain!

Tears that have no reason
Fall in my sorry heart:
What! there was no treason?
This grief hath no reason.

Nay! the more desolate,
Because, I know not why,
(Neither for love nor hate)
Mine heart is desolate.

AFTER PAUL VERLAINE

II

COLLOQUE SENTIMENTAL

Into the lonely park all frozen fast,
Awhile ago there were two forms who passed.

Lo, are their lips fallen and their eyes dead,
Hardly shall a man hear the words they said.

Into the lonely park, all frozen fast,
There came two shadows who recall the past.

"Dost thou remember our old ecstasy?"—
"Wherefore should I possess that memory?"—

"Doth thine heart beat at my sole name alway?
Still dost thou see my soul in visions?" "Nay!"—

"They were fair days of joy unspeakable,
Whereon our lips were joined?"—"I cannot tell."—

"Were not the heavens blue, was not hope high?"—
"Hope has fled vanquished down the darkling sky."—

So through the barren oats they wandered,
And the night only heard the words they said.

AFTER PAUL VERLAINE

III

SPLEEN

Around were all the roses red,
The ivy all around was black.

Dear, so thou only move thine head,
Shall all mine old despairs awake!

Too blue, too tender was the sky,
The air too soft, too green the sea.

Always I fear, I know not why,
Some lamentable flight from thee.

I am so tired of holly-sprays
And weary of the bright box-tree,

Of all the endless country ways;
Of everything alas! save thee.

AFTER PAUL VERLAINE

IV

The sky is up above the roof
    So blue, so soft!
A tree there, up above the roof,
    Swayeth aloft.

A bell within that sky we see,
    Chimes low and faint:
A bird upon that tree we see,
    Maketh complaint.

Dear God! is not the life up there,
    Simple and sweet?
How peacefully are borne up there
    Sounds of the street!

What hast thou done, who comest here,
    To weep alway?
Where hast thou laid, who comest here,
    Thy youth away?

TO HIS MISTRESS

There comes an end to summer,
  To spring showers and hoar rime;
His mumming to each mummer
  Has somewhere end in time,
And since life ends and laughter,
  And leaves fall and tears dry,
Who shall call love immortal,
  When all that is must die?

Nay, sweet, let's leave unspoken
  The vows the fates gainsay,
For all vows made are broken,
  We love but while we may.
Let's kiss when kissing pleases,
  And part when kisses pall,
Perchance, this time to-morrow,
  We shall not love at all.

You ask my love completest,
  As strong next year as now,
The devil take you, sweetest,
  Ere I make aught such vow.
Life is a masque that changes,
  A fig for constancy!
No love at all were better,
  Than love which is not free.

JADIS

Erewhile, before the world was old,
When violets grew and celandine,
In Cupid's train we were enrolled:
    Erewhile!
Your little hands were clasped in mine,
Your head all ruddy and sun-gold
Lay on my breast which was your shrine,
And all the tale of love was told:
Ah, God, that sweet things should decline,
And fires fade out which were not cold,
    Erewhile.

IN A BRETON CEMETERY

They sleep well here,
   These fisher-folk who passed their anxious days
   In fierce Atlantic ways;
And found not there,
   Beneath the long curled wave,
   So quiet a grave.

And they sleep well
   These peasant-folk, who told their lives away,
   From day to market-day,
As one should tell,
   With patient industry,
   Some sad old rosary.

And now night falls,
   Me, tempest-tost, and driven from pillar to post,
   A poor worn ghost,
This quiet pasture calls;
   And dear dead people with pale hands
   Beckon me to their lands.

TO WILLIAM THEODORE PETERS
ON HIS RENAISSANCE CLOAK

The cherry-coloured velvet of your cloak
  Time hath not soiled: its fair embroideries
Gleam as when centuries ago they spoke
  To what bright gallant of Her Daintiness,
    Whose slender fingers, long since dust and dead,
    For love or courtesy embroidered
The cherry-coloured velvet of this cloak.

Ah! cunning flowers of silk and silver thread,
  That mock mortality! the broidering dame,
The page they decked, the kings and courts are dead:
  Gone the age beautiful; Lorenzo's name,
    The Borgia's pride are but an empty sound;
    But lustrous still upon their velvet ground,
Time spares these flowers of silk and silver thread.

Gone is that age of pageant and of pride:
  Yet don your cloak, and haply it shall seem,
The curtain of old time is set aside;
  As through the sadder coloured throng you gleam;
    We see once more fair dame and gallant gay,
    The glamour and the grace of yesterday:
The elder, brighter age of pomp and pride.

THE SEA-CHANGE

Where river and ocean meet in a great tempestuous
    frown,
Beyond the bar, where on the dunes the white-capped
    rollers break;
Above, one windmill stands forlorn on the arid, grassy
    down:
I will set my sail on a stormy day and cross the bar and
    seek
That I have sought and never found, the exquisite one
    crown,
Which crowns one day with all its calm the passionate
    and the weak.

When the mad winds are unreined, wilt thou not
    storm, my sea?
(I have ever loved thee so, I have ever done thee
    wrong
In dear terrestrial ways.) When I trust myself to
    thee
With a last great hope, arise and sing thine ultimate,
    great song
Sung to so many better men, O sing at last to me,
That which when once a man has heard, he heeds not
    over long.

I will bend my sail when the great day comes; thy kisses
    on my face
Shall seal all things that are old, outworn; and anger
    and regret
Shall fade as the dreams and days shall fade, and in thy
    salt embrace,
When thy fierce caresses blind mine eyes and my limbs
    grow stark and set,
All that I know in all my mind shall no more have a
    place:
The weary ways of men and one woman I shall forget.

Point du Pouldu

DREGS

The fire is out, and spent the warmth thereof,
(This is the end of every song man sings!)
The golden wine is drunk, the dregs remain,
Bitter as wormwood and as salt as pain;
And health and hope have gone the way of love
Into the drear oblivion of lost things.
Ghosts go along with us until the end;
This was a mistress, this, perhaps, a friend.
With pale, indifferent eyes, we sit and wait
For the dropt curtain and the closing gate:
This is the end of all the songs man sings.

A SONG

All that a man may pray,
  Have I not prayed to thee?
What were praise left to say,
  Has not been said by me,
    O, *ma mie?*

Yet thine eyes and thine heart,
  Always were dumb to me:
Only to be my part,
  Sorrow has come from thee,
    O, *ma mie?*

Where shall I seek and hide
  My grief away with me?
Lest my bitter tears should chide,
  Bring brief dismay to thee,
    O, *ma mie?*

More than a man may pray,
  Have I not prayed to thee?
What were praise left to say,
  Has not been said by me,
    O, *ma mie?*

BRETON AFTERNOON

Here, where the breath of the scented-gorse floats through
    the sun-stained air,
On a steep hill-side, on a grassy ledge, I have lain hours
    long and heard
Only the faint breeze pass in a whisper like a prayer,
And the river ripple by and the distant call of a bird.

On the lone hill-side, in the gold sunshine, I will hush me
    and repose,
And the world fades into a dream and a spell is cast on
    me;
And what was all the strife about, for the myrtle or the rose,
And why have I wept for a white girl's paleness passing ivory!

Out of the tumult of angry tongues, in a land alone, apart,
In a perfumed dream-land set betwixt the bounds of life
    and death,
Here will I lie while the clouds fly by and delve an hole
    where my heart
May sleep deep down with the gorse above and red,
    red earth beneath.

Sleep and be quiet for an afternoon, till the rose-white
    angelus
Softly steals my way from the village under the hill:
Mother of God, O Misericord, look down in pity on us,
The weak and blind who stand in our light and wreak
    ourselves such ill.

VENITE DESCENDAMUS

Let be at last; give over words and sighing,
    Vainly were all things said:
Better at last to find a place for lying,
    Only dead.

Silence were best, with songs and sighing over;
    Now be the music mute;
Now let the dead, red leaves of autumn cover
    A vain lute.

Silence is best: for ever and for ever,
    We will go down and sleep,
Somewhere beyond her ken, where she need never
    Come to weep

Let be at last: colder she grows and colder;
    Sleep and the night were best;
Lying at last where we can not behold her,
    We may rest.

TRANSITION

A little while to walk with thee, dear child;
  To lean on thee my weak and weary head;
Then evening comes: the winter sky is wild,
  The leafless trees are black, the leaves long dead.

A little while to hold thee and to stand,
  By harvest-fields of bending golden corn:
Then the predestined silence, and thine hand,
  Lost in the night, long and weary and forlorn.

A little while to love thee, scarcely time
  To love thee well enough; then time to part,
To fare through wintry fields alone and climb
  The frozen hills, not knowing where thou art.

Short summer-time and then, my heart's desire,
  The winter and the darkness: one by one
The roses fall, the pale roses expire
  Beneath the slow decadence of the sun.

EXCHANGES

All that I had I brought,
  Little enough I know;
A poor rhyme roughly wrought,
  A rose to match thy snow:
All that I had I brought.

Little enough I sought:
  But a word compassionate,
A passing glance, or thought,
  For me outside the gate:
Little enough I sought.

Little enough I found:
  All that you had, perchance!
With the dead leaves on the ground,
  I dance the devil's dance.
All that you had I found.

TO A LADY ASKING FOOLISH QUESTIONS

Why am I sorry, Chloe? Because the moon is far:
And who am I to be straitened in a little earthly star?

Because thy face is fair? And what if it had not been,
The fairest face of all is the face I have not seen.

Because the land is cold, and however I scheme and plot,
I can not find a ferry to the land where I am not.

Because thy lips are red and thy breasts upbraid the
 snow?
(There is neither white nor red in the pleasance where
 I go.)

Because thy lips grow pale and thy breasts grow dun
 and fall?
I go where the wind blows, Chloe, and am not sorry
 at all.

RONDEAU

Ah, Manon, say, why is it we
Are one and all so fain of thee?
Thy rich red beauty debonnaire
In very truth is not more fair,
Than the shy grace and purity
That clothe the maiden maidenly;
Her gray eyes shine more tenderly
And not less bright than thine her hair,
   Ah, Manon, say!
Expound, I pray, the mystery
Why wine-stained lip and languid eye,
And most unsaintly Maenad air,
Should move us more than all the rare
White roses of virginity?
   Ah, Manon, say!

MORITURA

A song of the setting sun!
  The sky in the west is red,
And the day is all but done:
  While yonder up overhead,
    All too soon,
There rises, so cold, the cynic moon.

A song of a winter day!
  The wind of the north doth blow,
From a sky that's chill and gray,
  On fields where no crops now grow,
    Fields long shorn
Of bearded barley and golden corn.

A song of an old, old man!
  His hairs are white and his gaze,
Long bleared in his visage wan,
  With its weight of yesterdays,
    Joylessly
He stands and mumbles and looks at me.

A song of a faded flower!
  'Twas plucked in the tender bud,
And fair and fresh for an hour,
  In a lady's hair it stood.
    Now, ah, now,
Faded it lies in the dust and low.

LIBERA ME

Goddess the laughter-loving, Aphrodite befriend!
Long have I served thine altars, serve me now at the
    end,
Let me have peace of thee, truce of thee, golden one,
    send.

Heart of my heart have I offered thee, pain of my pain,
Yielding my life for the love of thee into thy chain;
Lady and goddess be merciful, loose me again.

All things I had that were fairest, my dearest and best,
Fed the fierce flames on thine altar: ah, surely, my
    breast
Shrined thee alone among goddesses, spurning the rest.

Blossom of youth thou hast plucked of me, flower of my
    days;
Stinted I nought in thine honouring, walked in thy
    ways,
Song of my soul pouring out to thee, all in thy praise.

Fierce was the flame while it lasted, and strong was
    thy wine,
Meet for immortals that die not, for throats such as
    thine,
Too fierce for bodies of mortals, too potent for mine.

Blossom and bloom hast thou taken, now render to me
Ashes of life that remain to me, few though they be,
Truce of the love of thee, Cyprian, let me go free.

Goddess, the laughter-loving, Aphrodite, restore
Life to the limbs of me, liberty, hold me no more
Having the first-fruits and flower of me, cast me the
    core.

TO A LOST LOVE

I seek no more to bridge the gulf that lies
   Betwixt our separate ways;
   For vainly my heart prays,
Hope droops her head and dies;
I see the sad, tired answer in your eyes.

I did not heed, and yet the stars were clear;
   Dreaming that love could mate
   Lives grown so separate;—
But at the best, my dear,
I see we should not have been very near.

I knew the end before the end was nigh:
   The stars have grown so plain;
   Vainly I sigh, in vain
For things that come to some,
But unto you and me will never come.

WISDOM

Love wine and beauty and the spring,
  While wine is red and spring is here,
And through the almond blossoms ring
  The dove-like voices of thy Dear.

Love wine and spring and beauty while
  The wine hath flavour and spring masks
Her treachery in so soft a smile
  That none may think of toil and tasks.

But when spring goes on hurrying feet,
  Look not thy sorrow in the eyes,
And bless thy freedom from thy sweet:
  This is the wisdom of the wise.

IN SPRING

See how the trees and the osiers lithe
Are green bedecked and the woods are blithe,
The meadows have donned their cape of flowers
The air is soft with the sweet May showers,
    And the birds make melody:
But the spring of the soul, the spring of the soul,
    Cometh no more for you or for me.

The lazy hum of the busy bees
Murmureth through the almond trees;
The jonquil flaunteth a gay, blonde head,
The primrose peeps from a mossy bed,
    And the violets scent the lane.
But the flowers of the soul, the flowers of the soul,
    For you and for me bloom never again.

A LAST WORD

Let us go hence: the night is now at hand;
The day is overworn, the birds all flown;
And we have reaped the crops the gods have sown;
Despair and death; deep darkness o'er the land,
Broods like an owl; we cannot understand
Laughter or tears, for we have only known
Surpassing vanity: vain things alone
Have driven our perverse and aimless band.
Let us go hence, somewhither strange and cold,
To Hollow Lands where just men and unjust
Find end of labour, where's rest for the old,
Freedom to all from love and fear and lust.
Twine our torn hands! O pray the earth enfold
Our life-sick hearts and turn them into dust.

IN PROSE

THE FORTUNATE ISLANDS

Bearded, with tawny faces, as they sat on the quay, looking listlessly at nothing with their travelled eyes, I questioned them:

"We have adventured," they said.

"Tell me of your travels, O mariners, of that you have sought and found, of high perils undergone and great salvage and of those fortunate islands which lie in a quiet sea, azure beyond my dreaming."

"We have found nothing. There is nothing saved," they said.

"But tell me, O mariners, for I have travelled a little. I have looked for the woman I might have loved, and the friend we hear of, and the country where I am not. Tell me of your discoveries."

One of them answered:

"We tell you the truth. We are old, withered mariners, and long and far have we wandered in the seas of no discovery. We have been to the end of the last ocean, but there was nothing, not even the things of which you speak. We have adventured, but we have not found anything, and here we are again in the port of our nativity, and there is only one thing we expect. Is it not so, comrades?"

Each raised a hand of asseveration; and they said:

"We tell you the truth: there are no fortunate islands."

And they fell into their old silence.

MARKETS

After an Old Nursery Rhyme

"Where are you going, beautiful maiden?"

"I am going to market, sir."

"And what do you take with you, beautiful maiden? Lilies out of your garden?   White milk, warm from the cow, little pats of yellow butter, new-laid eggs, this morning's mushrooms? Where is your basket? Why have you nothing in your hands?"

"I am going to market, sir."

"Beautiful maiden, may I come with you?"

"Oh, sir."

ABSINTHIA TAETRA

Green changed to white, emerald to an opal: nothing was changed.

The man let the water trickle gently into his glass, and as the green clouded, a mist fell away from his mind.

Then he drank opaline.

Memories and terrors beset him. The past tore after him like a panther and through the blackness of the present he saw the luminous tiger eyes of the things to be.

But he drank opaline.

And that obscure night of the soul, and the valley of humiliation, through which he stumbled were forgotten. He saw blue vistas of undiscovered countries, high prospects and a quiet, caressing sea. The past shed its perfume over him, to-day held his hand as it were a little child, and to-morrow shone like a white star: nothing was changed.

He drank opaline.

The man had known the obscure night of the soul, and lay even now in the valley of humiliation; and the tiger menace of the things to be was red in the skies. But for a little while he had forgotten.

Green changed to white, emerald to an opal: nothing was changed.

THE VISIT

As though I were still struggling through the meshes of some riotous dream, I heard his knock upon the door. As in a dream, I bade him enter, but with his entry, I awoke. Yet when he entered it seemed to me that I was dreaming, for there was nothing strange in that supreme and sorrowful smile which shone through the mask which I knew. And just as though I had not always been afraid of him I said: "Welcome."

And he said very simply, "I am here."

Dreaming I had thought myself, but the reproachful sorrow of his smile showed me that I was awake. Then dared I open my eyes and I saw my old body on the bed, and the room in which I had grown so tired, and in the middle of the room the pan of charcoal which still smouldered. And dimly I remembered my great weariness and the lost whiteness of Lalage and last year's snows; and these things had been agonies.

Darkly, as in a dream, I wondered why they gave me no more hurt, as I looked at my old body on the bed; why, they were like old maids' fancies (as I looked at my gray body on the bed of my agonies)—like silly toys of children that fond mothers lay up in lavender (as I looked at the twisted limbs of my old body), for these things had been agonies.

But all my wonder was gone when I looked again into the eyes of my guest, and I said:

"I have wanted you all my life."

Then said Death (and what reproachful tenderness was shadowed in his obscure smile):

"You had only to call."

THE PRINCESS OF DREAMS

Poor legendary princess! In her enchaunted tower of ivory, the liberator thought that she awaited him.

For once in a dream he had seen, as they were flowers de luce, the blue lakes of her eyes, had seemed to be enveloped in a tangle of her golden hair.

And he sought her through the countless windings of her forest for many moons, sought her through the morasses, sparing not his horse nor his sword. On his way he slew certain evil magicians and many of his friends, so that at his journey's end his bright sword was tarnished and his comeliness swart with mud. His horses he had not spared: their bones made a white track behind him in the windings of the forest: but he still bore her ransom, all the costly, graceful things stored in a cypress chest: massed pearls and amethysts and silks from Samarcand, Valance of Venice, and fine tapestry of Tyre. All these he brought with him to the gates of her ivory tower.

Poor legendary princess.

For he did not free her and the fustian porter took his treasure and broke his stained sword in two.

And who knows where he went, horseless and disarmed, through the morasses and the dark windings of her forest under the moonless night, dreaming of those blue lakes which were flowers de luce, her eyes? Who knows? For the fustian porter says nothing, being slow of wit.

But there are some who say that she had no wish to be freed, and that those flowers de luce, her eyes, are a stagnant, dark pool, that her glorious golden hair was only long enough to reach her postern gate.

Some say, moreover, that her tower is not of ivory and that she is not even virtuous nor a princess.

HITHERTO
UNPUBLISHED
POEMS

TO CYNARA

Ah take these songs my love, long time forgiven,
    Songs thou shalt never see,
Yet let them stand as a token that I am shriven,
    As thou by me?

The wrong is old, perchance could I approach thee,
    Eye speak to eye, who knows?—
It should fade as a mist—ah well, I cannot reproach
    thee—
      He reaps who sows.

Thou lovedst me once and I am still thy lover
    Fain of thee as of old
Fain of thy lips and thy locks that did ever hover
    Twixt brown and gold

    Ay woe is me

A MOSAIC

Dreams, dreams of a day gone by!
(Blue skies and the sunny south)
A fair small face and a rosebud mouth,
(O Love, my Love and Italy!)
As the moist fresh rain in a time of drouth,
She came, my Love, as a child to me.

Grey olives and sparkling sea
Shine bright through the clear calm air—
Of gleaming gold is her waving hair—
(O Love, my Love and Italy!)
When the world was young and the earth was fair,
She came, my Love, as a child to me.

Dreams, dreams of a day gone by!
(Grey eyes and a sunny smile)
Pure and a maiden and free from guile,
(O Love, my Love and Italy!)
In a dream she came and a little while
Tarried and went as a child from me.

White horses out on the sea,
Mist on the hills and a drizzling rain,
The wind wails loud like a soul in pain:—
(O Love, my Love and Italy!)
I called her long yet I call in vain,
Who came and went as a child from me.

REQUIEM

Encircle her head with a clustering wreath
Of lilies and roses and woodland flowers,
That she loved to pluck from garden and heath
When the Earth smelt fresh of sweet May showers,
And no sombre shade of sorrow had laid
A pitiless hand on her sunny hours.

Bring cowslips and violets and redolent may,
And daffodowndillies all yellow clad,
With the pale primrose, but never a spray
Of sorrowing yew or cypress sad
To shadow the grace of her peaceful face,
With aught that is gloomy or dull or grey.

For her life was a garden and she the pale
Queen lily that ruled all that fair emprise.
So weave her of flowers a maiden veil,
That Death may not see her dear grey eyes,
And hold her for aye, in his hut of clay,
Where no sun shines and the stars never rise.

Then one last long kiss on her beautiful hair,
And one last long look at her shapely head,—
Soft—turn away and shed never a tear,
For the purest soul that ever sped,
From a world of dust to her rest we trust—
Nay—what is life that ye weep for the dead?

POTNIA THEA

When the voice of the gods hath spoken,
    The uttered word remains,
The Parcae's web unbroken,
    Its pristine strength retains.

Tho' the Cronian Zeus be dethronèd
    And desolate his shrines,
Anangkè still star-crownèd.
    Her fateful threads entwines.

Tho' the goddess, the Cytherean,
    No longer with the Loves
Flits o'er the blue Aegean
    To hallowed Paphos' groves.

And Athênê has ceased enfolding
    The city of her heart,
Its denizens beholding
    The Delian barque depart,

Still the iconoclastic ages
    Touch not the veilèd dame
Whom husbandmen and sages
    Avouch by different name.

The Olympian queen's forgotten,
   Hephaestus' fires are cold,
The sons of Zeus begotten,
   The heroes rest untold.

Not a sound on the steep Cithaeron,
   Where once the Maenad's choir,
Adored the mighty Bromian,
   With dithyrambic fire.

Still the throne of Anangkè resteth
   Above the reach of years;
Her crape-crowned sceptre breasteth
   The ages without fears.

And when dynasties have been changed
   Of earths and gods and men,
The goddess unestrangèd
   Shall be found ruling then.

RONDEAU

Could you forget, put out of mind,
The vows you made, O most unkind?
The sweet love songs, the fair and frail
Lip utterance without avail,
The pleasure that you used to find,
Or said you found when passion blind,
I kissed the hand that you resigned,
Not all unwilling, maiden pale.
    Tho' you forget!
Where once our sunny paths entwined
There bloweth now the wintry wind:—
Ah dreamt we then time would assail,
Our trust and troth or love could fail,
In those old days that lie behind,
    That you forget?

RONDEAU

In Autumn when the leaf is sere,
In that still season of the year,
Shall we not meet once more we twain,
Who parted in the Spring of pain?
With eyes of passion long grown clear,
When youth is gone and Winter near,
May we not meet once more my dear,
Touch hands, forgive and part again,
  In Autumn?
Tho' bitter anger still doth blear,
The glory of the days that were,

   * * *

In rare still hours are you not fain
To cry a truce to dear disdain,
  In Autumn?

SONNETS

I

IN MEMORIAM. H.C. *ob*. Feb. 24, 1886

I have no heart to wish thee back again
To this sick earth, poor friend, who may have found,
Beneath the kind cold shelter of the ground
That calm memorial light that with much pain,
Thou lost in thy last years and sought in vain.
Nay it is better thus! thy life is crowned
Tho' but in death with peace—no jarring sound
Shall ever break the sleep wherein thou'rt lain.
Yet when I mournfully recall to mind
The fragrant summer days I spent with thee
In such calm unison and how thy kind
Unruffled cheerfulness would oftimes free
My mind from brooding thought I look behind
And fall before the shrine of memory.

II

NOVALIS

It has grown evening around me while I was looking into the red of morning.

NOVALIS

Ay—even so—fixt was that ardent gaze
Upon the East—his eagle eyes broad scanned
The vault of heaven and all the outlying land,
Shadowed in rose and amber neath the rays
Born of the rising sun,—a day of days
Was dawning for him mystical and grand,
His budding hopes the morning soft breeze fanned,
The future lay enwrapped in golden haze.
A moment—and the loveliness is gone!
Faded the glamour of morning from his sight,
Faded the quivering radiance that shone
On sea and shore and clothed the hills in light.
A sombre shade of evening settled down
And in the gathering gloom he stood alone.

OF A LITTLE GIRL

(1)

When life doth languish midst the bitter wrong
That riots everywhere, when all hopes fail,
And comfort is most weak and doubt most strong,
And friends are false and woman's troth proves frail,
And all thy soul for very life-sickness
Doth long to end, there yet is one sweet thing,
One fresh oasis in the wilderness
Of this sad world whereunto thou shalt cling
As to salvation—a child's tender love.
Ah do not doubt it—all things die and wane,
Save this alone; this only lasts above,
The lingering rule of weariness and pain,
This love alone is stingless and can calm
Life's fitful fever with its healing balm.

OF A LITTLE GIRL

(II)

Was it at even, with the casement thrown
Wide to the summer air, I sat and thought,
Of that ideal which I ever sought,
But fruitlessly—and so was fain to moan—
"Ah weariness of waiting thus alone,
With vanity of living all distraught,
To find upon the earth nor peace nor aught
Lovely or pure, whence all things sweet have gone."
And then one passed the dark'ning road along
And lit it with her childhood, that I felt
Passion and bitterness like snowflakes melt
Before the sun, and into praise and song
From the despair wherein it long had dwelt
My life burst flower-like and my soul grew strong.

OF A LITTLE GIRL

(III)

The music in a name, who can conceive,
Who may define?   Ah child thou dost not know
How many a time when my life's lamp burns low
And hope's light flickers—thou wouldst not believe
How thy dear treasured name will oft relieve
My sinking heart, how sweetly soft and low
My lips will frame it loath to let it go,
And kiss it quietly till I cease to grieve.
It is mine amulet, wrought rich and rare
With lovely fantasies, it is a charm
That whispered gently guardeth me from harm,
It is my ritual, my mystic prayer,
And in the hush of night thro' lattice bars
I see it written in the lonely stars.

OF A LITTLE GIRL

(IV)

Even as a child whose eager fingers snatch
An ocean shell and hold it to his ear,
With wondering, awe-struck eyes is hushed to catch
The murmurous music of its coilèd sphere;
Whispers of wind and wave, soul-stirring songs
Of storm-tossed ships and all the mystery
That to the illimitable sea belongs,
Stream to him from its tiny cavity.
As such an one with reverent awe I hold
Thy tender hand, and in those pure grey eyes,
That sweet child face, those tumbled curls of gold,
And in thy smiles and loving, soft replies
I find the whole of love—hear full and low
Its mystic ocean's tremulous ebb and flow.

OF A LITTLE GIRL

(v)

When it is over—when the final fight
Has been out-fought and the last moisty clod
Rattles upon my coffin, when the sod
Seals me for ever in that land of night
Whence joy and pain have ta'en impartial flight,
And the old lanes my feet so oft have trod
Know me no more but all men toil and plod
Over my head, my name forgotten quite.
Wilt thou sometimes—not often—God forfend
That thought of me should chase away thy smile
Or dull thy gladness, yet once in a while
Dream of a day departed and a friend
Who placed above the world and Fortune's prize
The love that centred in thy childish eyes.

OF A LITTLE GIRL

(VI)

For the last time, perhaps for weary years
Perhaps for ever, I have looked upon
Thy fair fair face;—those grey eyes that have shone
Such comfort on me when the foul fiend fear's
Gaunt haggard laugh would mock me and hot tears
For very loathing of my life rain down,
That trusting smile the one thing sweet I've known
I' the bitterness of life—all disappears.
Farewell, dear saint, I leave thee and I lay
No tax upon thy memory though God knows
This sobbing sea that sadly ebbs and flows
Shall not more surely each returning day
Cling to the callous shore than I in thee
Behold my drear life's dearest memory

OF A LITTLE GIRL

(VII)

So—it is finished and I cannot weep
Nor rave nor utter moan, life is too strong
For my weak will, it carries me along
On its fierce current till I fain would creep
Into some cavern still and fall asleep
And sleeping die, or melt like a sad song
Into the winds—I care not to hold long
This dreary life where pain alone is deep.
O child, my child, forgive me, I am vain,
Unworthy of thy love, I will not task
Even thy pity, who have ta'en a mask
And shall not show my living face again,
Until the end of all things joy and pain
Has given me more than now I dare to ask.

OF A LITTLE GIRL

(VIII) EPILOGUE

[Let us go hence: the night is now at hand;
The day is overworn, the birds all flown;
And we have reaped the crops the gods have sown;
Despair and death; deep darkness o'er the land,
Broods like an owl; we cannot understand
Laughter or tears, for we have only known
Surpassing vanity: vain things alone
Have driven our perverse and aimless band.
Let us go hence, somewhither strange and cold,
To Hollow Lands where just men and unjust
Find end of labour, where's rest for the old,
Freedom to all from love and fear and lust.
Twine our torn hands!   O pray the earth enfold
Our life-sick hearts and turn them into dust.]

LA JEUNESSE N'A QU'UN TEMPS

Swiftly passes youth away
Night is coming, fades the day,
All things turn to sombre grey.

Pass the cup and drink, friends, deep
Roses upon roses heap,
Soon it will be time to sleep.

Man, poor man, is born to die,
Love and all things fair will fly
Fill the cup and drain it dry.

Make ye merry, while ye may;
Snatch the sweetness of the day,
Pluck life's pleasures while they stay

When our youth has taken flight,
When the day is lost in night,
There can be no more delight.

Here's a glass to memory
Here's to death and vanity,
Here's a glass to you and me.

SONG OF THE XIXTH CENTURY

O send us light!
More light, more light and fuller clearer day,
We mortals moan and shudder at the night,
And ever still the shadows grow more grey,
    The stars less bright.

O give us faith—
In God, Man, anything to rise and break
The mists of doubt, we cry, but like a wraith
It still eludes our grasp and no rays streak
    The dark of Death.

O give us rest!
We all unrestful sigh, we ask not joy
Who stand with tearless eyes by life opprest,—
Joy turns to pain and love and sorrow cloy,
    But Peace is best.

A LULLABY

Sleep soundly, my pretty child,
    Sleep, sleep on
And all things fearful and all things wild
Far, far from thy pillow begone,
    Dream of the morrow,
Thou shalt not wake to weep
    Unknowing of sorrow,
O sleep, my little one, dream and sleep.

Sleep softly, my darling sleep!
    Soon, too soon
Dawneth the day when thou canst weep,
Weep, wail for the joy that is flown,
    Wearily yearning,
For love that is passed away,
    For peace unreturning.

SPLEEN

In the dull dark days of our life
We wander without a goal;
And the plague of living and strife
Eats worm-like into our soul.

To the tune of sighing and tears,
A weary purposeless band,
For the destined desolate years,
We fare thro' the Hopeless land.

On our lips are signs as of fire,
Our eyes are wild with despair,
We are burnt with a fierce desire
For that we know not nor care.

SPLEEN

With loathing of life that is past,
With horror of days to be,
We shiver like leaves in the blast,
Neath the breath of memory

In the tearing fangs of remorse
We are fain to fall in the mire,
And wallowing seek for the source,
Of the Lethe we desire.

Yet still are we troubled and torn,
By ennui, spleen and regret,
Whatever the depths of our scorn,
We cannot hope to forget.

O man, poor pitiful worm,
Foul nature's filthiest spawn,
As the helmless ship in a storm
So *thou* from the day thou art born

AFTER MANY YEARS

Sleep on dear now!
With thy golden hair that flows
On thy calm, thy icy brow
And thy close shut eyes, I trow
The sounds of my song cannot move thee now.
As they moved thee little in life—God knows.

Time was of old,
I did lull thee on my knee,
And thy locks of rippling gold
Streamed on my arm that did enfold,
And rocked thee to sleep who wast not so cold,
As thou liest now in Death's mystery.

How many years
Have waned since that distant day,
Seen dim thro' a mist of tears?
How many cycles of years?
Answer me, child, for I have my fears
That it was not real but part of a play.

Is it a dream
To see thee so calm and cold,
Who when I knew thee did seem
Never more still than the stream?
Or is it part real and partly a dream
Or a dream or in part the days of old?

Have I grown grey?
Or can it be I am dead.
And in spite of all they say,
And all I myself have said,
It is not all done with the very dead,
When the light of this life is worn away?

Nay it is true!
And I cannot doubt dear heart,
That this is really you.
'Tis too sad not to be true
And I mind me now it was this I knew
When the high gods had it that we should part.

You pay no heed,
And I will not linger long
For I trow you have no need
Still to be lulled by my song.
Now you sleep so sound and will sleep so long
You can do without me in very deed.

PRAETERITA

O childish forms and faces
That live in memorie's shrine;
O pleasant paths and places
That small feet trod with mine,
The old days that are dying
Soft melodies are sighing
Of something that is lying,
Pale in the past behind

The laughter that rejoices
Responds not to our quest,
The tender children's voices,
Are long time hushed to rest,
And all the stress of ages,
And all the love of sages
Can not return the pages
That life has once down pressed.

Before us dawns the vista
Of all our days to be,
But shall we find, my sister,
The charm that used to be
We know now to our sorrow,
The sad and strange to morrow,
Can never never borrow
The old time mystery.

When you and I did wander
On straying childish feet,
Before us lying yonder
The hills so strange and sweet;
When life was in the dawning,
The fair and golden morning
Sent unto us no warning
To stay the years' deceit.

The golden light has faded
That met our dazzled eyes,
The purple hills are shaded,
And leaden clouds arise;
And spring of childhood's gladness
And youth's brief summer madness
Has yielded to the sadness
Of dull autumnal skies.

ADIOS!

My sweet child-love, farewell!
My little tender flower
Who comforted me long and well,
In many a hope-deserted hour,
I bid thee now farewell.

The years shall come and go
And thro' thy village home,
The rippling streamlet still shall flow,
While far away my footsteps roam,
Who bid thee now farewell.

O sweet, O saintly face,
And innocent grey eyes,
That shone with such pathetic grace,
Wherein such dreamy wisdom lies,
I bid you now farewell.

Flow on, dear life in peace,
In peace and purity,
And all my life I shall not cease,
To hold thee shrined in memory,
Who bid thee now farewell.

SERAPHITA—SERAPHITUS

I seek for thee, I call thee, O my darling
In the land of wild unrest,
Very fain I were to see thee and to hold thee
And be pillowed on thy breast.

All my early hopes and faiths have long time failed me,
And this life of ours doth seem
In the deathless sleep that hems the world on both sides
But an evil passing dream

Yet I long for thee, thou one form pure and perfect,
In the seething obscene throng,
Just to hold thee for one instant and to know thee,
Then to part and pass along.

It would help me on the dreary path before me,
On the road thro Life to Death,
To have met thee once, belovèd, ere I hie me
To my home the earth beneath.

Somewhere tho' I know thee not, I know thou dwellest,
Somewhere on the earth, my queen,
Thou art sitting waiting for me fond and faithful,
Tho' a whole world flow between.

And I send these songs out to thee from the shadows,
And I call to thee and cling,
Who are shrinèd tho' perchance I never find thee,
In whatever song I sing.

IT IS FINISHED

The pure grey eyes are closèd now,
They shall not look on yours again;
Upon that pale and perfect brow,
There stays no sign of grief or pain.

The little face is white and cold,
The parted lips give forth no breath,
The grape-like curls of sun-bleached gold,
Are clammy with the dews of death.

Speak to her and she will not hear,
Caress her, but she will not move,
No longer feels she hope or fear,
No longer knows she hate or love.

Ah dream no false or futile dreams,
Nor lull thyself on fantasy,
That death is other than it seems,
Or leads to immortality.

She will not speak to thee again,
Tho' thy whole soul in tears be shed,
For tears and prayers are all in vain,
She is but dead, she is but dead!

ERE I GO HENCE

Ere I go hence and am no longer seen,
Ere I go hence into the dark of death,
And leave my body and my vital breath,
While over me the grass grows dank and green,
Let me behold thee, let me once again
Press thy fair palm, my fairest without stain,
  Ere I go hence.

Ere I go hence and leave this upper light,
Ere I go hence into the deathless sleep
That lies beyond the land, where cold and deep,
The stream of Lethe flows thro' endless night,
Let me once more, my sweet child love, behold
Thy pure grey eyes, thy tresses of bright gold—
  Ere I go hence.

Ere I go hence and cast away all pain,
Ere I go hence and falter and forget
The fever and the madness and regret
That make all life, all love so passing vain—
O my heart's darling, let me hear once more
The music of thy step upon the floor,
  Ere I go hence.

TRANSIT GLORIA

A gleam thro' the darkness
Of years and of days,
A transient lifting
Of misery's haze !

A sound of soft music,
A momentary lull,
Of this foul gnawing ennui,
Then all things grow dull.

A rift in life's shadow,
Brief even as vain,
The madness of pleasure,
The sadness of pain.

A dream of hope crownèd
In days of despair;
A vision of beauty
In Vanity Fair.

Like sweet children's voices,
To one usèd long,
To harsh-laughing harlots'
Lascivious song.

Like snow-drops in winter,
Like soft summer rain,
Like sleep to the weary
And harassed by pain.

Like long cherished memories,
Death-white with regret,
Too sad to remember,
Too sweet to forget.

Dreams of what might have been
Ere terrors were rife,
A pause in the passion,
The fever of life.

A verdant oasis,
With all around sand,
A gush of blue violets,
The touch of a hand.

A meeting, a parting,
For æons and years;
A smile changing quickly
To passionate tears.

Ah gone is the phantom
Of hope and delight,
And faded the vision
In infinite night.

Life's wave bears me onward
A rudderless bark;
Somewhere in the future,
Death looms in the dark.

The current flows faster,
Loud waileth the wind;
All sweet things and faces
Fade fainter behind.

The end cometh surely,
And each weary wave
Brings nearer and nearer,
The haven, the grave.

And soon from her labour,
Tired mem'ry will cease
And infinite slumber
Bring infinite peace.

'Twas but for a moment
This rift thro' the days,
This transient lifting
Of misery's haze.

SONNET

TO NATURE

MORITURI TE SALUTANT

Thou unclean harpy, odorous of despair,
I offer up no praises on the shrine
Of thy wild beauty; thou art not divine,
Nor reverent at all thy tranquil air;
I know thee, evil one, and I am ware
Of all thy vileness;—never song of mine
Shall swell the shameful triumphs that are thine
Thou shalt not cajole me of ev'n one prayer.
O false, foul mother who to sate thy lust,
Insatiate of misery doth consume
The lives that thou hast fashioned out of dust,
Who feedest on the children of thy womb,
Thy beauty cannot conquer our distrust,
Thy tenderness is crueller than a tomb.

AWAKENING

We have dreamt dreams but now they are long over,
Dreams of a life the other side of death;
Drop down the curtain on the play completed,
The farce of life is finished with the breath.

We have believed the beautiful, false stories,
Fed on the faiths that after childhood fail,
Now to our eyes the universe appeareth
A vessel rudderless without a sail.

Man, in a world but fair in semblance only
Veiling in light its secret of disgust,
Is he not far of all vile things the vilest,
He, the foul spawn of Nature's filthy lust?

Man with his hopes and pitiful illusions,
Is he not pitiful, grotesque, forlorn?
White with desire for that life cannot proffer,
Must we not weep that ever we were born?

Is there one happy?   Can there be one happy?
Nay, for the only good we can attain,
Death our dull goal, the senseless sleep for ever
Puts alike end to pleasure and to pain.

There shall we rest, but shall not ever know it,
Shall not have love nor knowledge, nor delight,
Only shall feel the fevered life fall from us,
Sleepers unwitting in an endless night.

LULLABY

Blow soft thou summer wind,
Rough be not nor unkind,
Whisper outside the room,
Where in the peaceful gloom,
    My darling lies a-sleeping.
Let thy soft lullabies
Shut the dear innocent eyes
Of my child who lies a-sleeping.
Stream on ye pale moon-beams,
Light up her childish dreams,
Flow round her small white bed
Halo her golden head—
    My darling lies a-sleeping.
Let her repose be sound,
Wrap her in peace around,
My child who lies a-sleeping.

Hush, hush, thou unkind life,
Tumid and full of strife,
Let her sleep tranquilly,
Let her white childhood be,
My sweet who lies a-sleeping.
Save her soft eyes from tears
And the bitter love of years,—
My child who lies a-sleeping.

THE OLD YEAR

We stand at the end of the old year,
On the threshold of the new,
And we turn to the old year dying,
And shrink from the strange and new;
Ah, all fair children, welcome
The strong, young year that is born,
For us, who are no more children,
Who have little to do with morn,
We will sit, old year, in the firelight,
And see the last of you.

There you lie, with your sick, scarred visage,
Who were once so fair to see,
And the death-dew clings to your forehead,
And your breath draws painfully:—
In accents low you tell us,
How there is one end to all,
How love endures for a season,
How mirth departs in the fall—
As the day is, so the tomorrow,
As it has been, it shall be.

Where are they, the loves and passions
Of the old, sad year that dies?
They are dead, they are gone, forgotten
More swift than the summer skies;—
The tears, the song, the laughter,—
Ah say, were they worth regret?
Old year, is it kind or cruel,
That we wander and forget
The good and the ill we gather
From every year that dies?

Nay we wish thee well, we forgive thee,
And ywis that this is true,—
There are fairer days in the old years
Than ever dawn in the new!
What if we find fresh faces
In the young new year that dawns,
A guerdon of joy or sorrow,
A crown of laurel or thorns,—
There are sweeter things in the old years
Than ever come with the new.

THE NEW YEAR

The bells ring out, the year is born,
And shall we hope or shall we mourn?
Shall we embrace the young, new year,
Or shall we turn back lingering eyes,
    To the low bier,
Where in his pall the old year lies?

What shall he bring to men who weep,
To men who laugh and men who sleep,
So very weary of the sun?
Shall one of these men ever gain,
    Ah even one,
His heart's desire nor find it vain?

Hope not, fear not: he only bears
The message of the elder years!
A little love, a little pain!
To some a sweet or idle dream,
    To some again,
The sleep wherein we do not dream.

Ah sweet, my child, and yet mine own,
Though I must wander on alone,
Love me a little, clasp me still
With thy soft hands, and I will bear
    For good or ill
The burden of the coming year.

FROM THE ICELANDIC

Long time ago, I vowed to the Sea,
    My destined wife,
My one desire, I will give thee my life
    To hold of me:
For others the green, the daedal earth
My joy, my sorrow, my tears, my mirth
    Be thine O Sea!

They called me fickle, they called me cold,
    My human loves—
Cried: "His fancy moves as the salt sea moves",
    Who were not told,
How thy bitter kisses held my heart,
Sealed thine forever and set apart
    My bride, my Sea!

O changeful one! I cried to the Sea,
    O changeless one!
I forget me all things beneath the Sun,
    When rocked by thee.
Thine anger woos me, thy tempests thrill,
For am I not thine, to do thy will
    O Sea, my Sea?

And now thou art risen to prove my vows,
   My wooing done,
I was ever thy lover—, shall I shun
   To be thy spouse?
Was it not this that I knew before,
Waited and yearned for, when I swore
   To wed the Sea?

So!—comfort me, cool me, shed thy breath,
   Spare no embrace;
Ah lean thy brow over me, shroud my face,
   Kiss me to Death;
I am one with thee, O most sweet, held fast,
Made thine for ever, thy spouse at last,
   O Sea, my Sea!

LOVE'S EPILOGUE

When summer dies
There's an end of singing;
Dumb tears are springing
To wistful eyes,
At the death of summer
When the swallow flies,
His swift course winging
To softer skies.

Ev'n so, most sweet,
Is song time departed,
And we are parted,
As was most meet,
At the death of summer,
At the year's defeat,
To cry sad hearted,
That love is fleet.

Now all is said,
It were ill to tarry,
With tears to harry,
Love that is dead.
In the chill of autumn,
When the leaves are shed,
His corse we carry,
To earth, his bed.

Ah, look not there,
To where Love reposes!
Till tired life closes,
Be fain! Beware!
In the chill of autumn,—
Ah, forget thee where
With rue and roses,
Thou hid'st Love's bier

RONDEAU

HÉLÈNE

You loved me once! I charge you, sweet,
Leave me this last, one faith—in spite
Of broken vows and time's deceit,
     You loved me once!
What tho' I sit in utter night
And hear the swift, departing feet
Of young desires that take their flight,
And mourn that love should be so fleet,
And weep that you should prove so light,
The time has been I was complete,—
     You loved me once!

ROUNDEL

To HÉLÈNE

The golden hours! Ah, prithee, art not fain
Sometimes to drop a tear for their dead sake,
Who were so fair, to yearn for them again,
    The golden hours?
Could I forget them? Not though I should take
Of Lethe and Nepenthe for my pain;
I shall remember, sleeping and awake,
While life is life, my love and thy disdain—
Nay, though I die, methinks, I shall not slake
The thirst wherewith my soul recalls in vain
    The golden hours!

RONDEL

Ah, dear child, in whose kiss
Is healing of my pain,
Since life has given me this,
I will no more complain.
My heart to life, ywis,
Thy clinging hands enchain,
Ah, dear child in whose kiss,
Is healing of my pain.
Love me—I shall not miss
Old loves that did but stain,
Thy blue eyes teach me bliss,—
I am not all in vain,
Ah, dear child, in whose kiss
Is healing of my pain.

Discedam, explebo numerum, reddarque tenebris,
I decus, i, nostrum; melioribus utere fatis.

Because my life is an unworthy thing
Outworn and mildewed, I am dismayed,
I dare not give it thee, O child! O maid!
Too late divined, too sweet for me to sing:
Surely, my barren days I may not bring,
But rather giftless come, lest any shade
Or prescience of autumn should be laid
Upon thy fair life in its blossoming.
Yet would I give thee all, who stand aside,
Giving thee naught: yea! gladly lie down dead
That haply coming, where the roads divide
On lilies still thy tender feet might tread,
In daisied ways of innocence abide,
Until thy tale of days is reckoned.

AGAINST MY LADY BURTON: ON HER BURNING THE LAST WRITING OF HER DEAD HUSBAND

"To save his soul", whom narrowly she loved
She did this deed of everlasting shame,
For devils' laughter; and was soulless proved
Heaping dishonour on her scholar's name.
Her lean distrust awoke when he was dead;
Dead, hardly cold; whose life was worn away
In scholarship's high service; from his head
She lightly tore his ultimate crown of bay.
His masterpiece, the ripe fruit of his age,
In art's despite she gave the hungry flame;
Smiled at the death of each laborious page,
Which she read only by the light of shame.
Dying he trusted her: him dead she paid
Most womanly, destroying his life's prize:
So Judas decently his Lord betrayed
With deep dishonour wrought in love's disguise.
With deep dishonour, for her jealous heart
His whole life's work, with light excuse put by
For love of him, or haply, hating art.
Oh Love be this, let us curse Love and die.
Nay! Love forgive: could such a craven thing
Love anywhere? but let her name pass down
Dishonoured through the ages, who did fling
To the rank scented mob a sage's crown,
And offered Fame, Love, Honour, mincingly
To her one God—sterile Propriety!

THE REQUITAL

Because I am idolatrous, and have besought,
With grievous supplication, and consuming prayer,
The admirable image; that my dreams have wrought,
Out of her swan's neck and her dark, abundant hair;
The jealous gods that brook no worship save their own,
Turn my live idol marble, and her heart—a stone!

A LETTER FROM M.M.
VERSIFIED OUT OF POOR PROSE
INTO CATCHPENNY VERSE!

Dear Sir! would you be popular,
    Then never mention Greek!
Be arrogant and insular,
    Dear Sir, would you be popular:
Cut classics; and for guiding star,
Read Birrell once a week.
Dear Sir! would you be popular,
    Then never mention Greek.
                    Lionel Johnson.

In the days of the good, gay people,
Of the little folk in green,
The Moon shone clear in Fairyland,
Or ever the world was seen.

In vain we cross the seas change lands,
In search of that we know not

HITHERTO
UNCOLLECTED
POEMS

THE PASSING OF TENNYSON

As his own Arthur fared across the mere,
With the grave Queen, past knowledge of the throng,
Serene and calm, rebuking grief and tear,
Departs this prince of song.

Whom the gods love Death doth not cleave nor smite,
But like an angel, with soft trailing wing,
He gathers them upon the hush of night,
With voice and beckoning.

The moonlight falling on that august head
Smoothed out the mark of time's defiling hand,
And hushed the voice of mourning round his bed—
"He goes to his own land".

Beyond the ramparts of the world where stray
The laureled few o'er fields Elysian,
He joins his elders of the lyre and bay,
Led by the Mantuan.

We mourn him not, but sigh with Bedivere,
Not perished be the sword he bore so long,
Excalibur, whom none is left to wear—
His magic brand of song.

FANTASIE TRISTE

To my first love
Loved all above;
In late spring;
Pansies, pansies
Such strange fancies
Was all I had to bring.

To my last love
Loved all above:
At evening
Of autumn
One chrysanthemum
Is all I have to bring.

O first, be last
In a dim past!
With the dead flowers
And the strayed hours
There are no flowers left to bring
There are no songs left to sing
Let be at last.

THE PIERROT
OF THE MINUTE

A DRAMATIC PHANTASY
IN ONE ACT

THE CHARACTERS

A MOON MAIDEN

PIERROT

THE SCENE

A glade in the Parc du Petit Trianon. In the centre a Doric temple with steps coming down the stage. On the left a little Cupid on a pedestal. Twilight.

(Pierrot enters with his hands full of lilies. He is burdened with a little basket. He stands gazing at the Temple and the Statue.)

Pierrot.

My journey's end! This surely is the glade
Which I was promised: I have well obeyed!
A clue of lilies was I bid to find,
Where the green alleys most obscurely wind;
Where tall oaks darkliest canopy o'erhead,
And moss and violet make the softest bed;
Where the path ends, and leagues behind me lie
The gleaming courts and gardens of Versailles;
The lilies streamed before me, green and white;
I gathered, following: they led me right,   10
To the bright temple and the sacred grove:
This is, in truth, the very shrine of Love!

(He gathers together his flowers and lays them at the foot of Cupid's statue; then he goes timidly up the first steps of the temple and stops.)

Pierrot.

It is so solitary, I grow afraid.
Is there no priest here, no devoted maid?
Is there no oracle, no voice to speak,
Interpreting to me the word I seek?

(A very gentle music of lutes floats out from the temple. Pierrot starts back; he shows extreme

surprise; then he returns to the foreground, and
crouches down in rapt attention until the music
ceases. His face grows puzzled and petulant.)

Pierrot.

Too soon! too soon! in that enchanting strain,
Days yet unlived, I almost lived again:
It almost taught me that I most would know—
Why am I here, and why am I Pierrot?   20

(Absently he picks up a lily which has fallen to the
ground, and repeats:)

Pierrot.

Why came I here, and why am I Pierrot?
That music and this silence both affright;
Pierrot can never be a friend of night.
I never felt my solitude before—
Once safe at home, I will return no more.
Yet the commandment of the scroll was plain;
While the light lingers let me read again.

(He takes a scroll from his bosom and reads:)

Pierrot.

"*He loves to-night who never loved before;
Who ever loved, to-night shall love once more.*"
I never loved! I know not what love is.   30
I am so ignorant—but what is this?

(Reads)

" *Who would adventure to encounter Love*
Must rest one night within this hallowed grove.
Cast down thy lilies, which have led thee on,
Before the tender feet of Cupidon."
Thus much is done, the night remains to me.
Well, Cupidon, be my security!
Here is more writing, but too faint to read.

(He puzzles for a moment, then casts the scroll
down.)

Pierrot.

 Hence, vain old parchment. I have learnt thy
  rede!

(He looks round uneasily, starts at his shadow;
then discovers his basket with glee. He takes out
a flask of wine, pours it into a glass, and drinks.)

Pierrot.

 Courage, mon Ami! I shall never miss   40
Society with such a friend as this.
How merrily the rosy bubbles pass,
Across the amber crystal of the glass.
I had forgotten you. Methinks this quest
Can wake no sweeter echo in my breast.

(Looks round at the statue, and starts.)

Pierrot.

> Nay, little god! forgive.   I did but jest.

(He fills another glass, and pours it upon the statue.)

Pierrot.

> This libation, Cupid, take,
>> With the lilies at thy feet;
> Cherish Pierrot for their sake
>> Send him visions strange and sweet,   50
> While he slumbers at thy feet.
> Only love kiss him awake!
>> *Only love kiss him awake!*

(Slowly falls the darkness, soft music plays, while Pierrot gathers together fern and foliage into a rough couch at the foot of the steps which lead to the Temple d'Amour.   Then he lies down upon it, having made his prayer.   It is night.)

Pierrot.   (Softly.)

> Music, more music, far away and faint:
> It is an echo of mine heart's complaint.
> Why should I be so musical and sad?
> I wonder why I used to be so glad?
> In single glee I chased blue butterflies,
> Half butterfly myself, but not so wise,
> For they were twain, and I was only one.   60
> Ah me! how pitiful to be alone.

My brown birds told me much, but in mine ear
They never whispered this—I learned it here:
The soft wood sounds, the rustlings in the breeze,
Are but the stealthy kisses of the trees.
Each flower and fern in this enchanted wood
Leans to her fellow, and is understood;
The eglantine, in loftier station set,
Stoops down to woo the maidly violet.
In gracile pairs the very lilies grow: 70
None is companionless except Pierrot.
Music, more music! how its echoes steal
Upon my senses with unlooked for weal.
Tired am I, tired, and far from this lone glade
Seems mine old joy in rout and masquerade.
Sleep cometh over me, now will I prove,
By Cupid's grace, what is this thing called love.

(Sleeps.)

(There is more music of lutes for an interval, during
which a bright radiance, white and cold, streams from
the temple upon the face of Pierrot. Presently a
Moon Maiden steps out of the temple; she descends
and stands over the sleeper.)

The Lady.

    Who is this mortal
      Who ventures to-night
    To woo an immortal,   80
      Cold, cold the moon's light,

For sleep at this portal,
  Bold lover of night.
Fair is the mortal
  In soft, silken white,
Who seeks an immortal.
  Ah, lover of night,
Be warned at the portal,
  And save thee in flight!

(She stoops over him: Pierrot stirs in his sleep.)

Pierrot (Murmuring).

Forget not, Cupid. Teach me all thy lore: 90
"*He loves to-night who never loved before.*"

The Lady.

  Unwitting boy! when, be it soon or late,
What Pierrot ever has escaped his fate?
What if I warned him! He might yet evade,
Through the long windings of this verdant glade;
Seek his companions in the blither way,
Which, else, must be as lost as yesterday.
So might he still pass some unheeding hours
In the sweet company of birds and flowers.
How fair he is, with red lips formed for joy,   100
As softly curved as those of Venus' boy.
Methinks his eyes, beneath their silver sheaves,
Rest tranquilly like lilies under leaves.
Arrayed in innocence, what touch of grace
Reveals the scion of a courtly race?

Well, I will warn him, though, I fear, too late—
What Pierrot ever has escaped his fate?
But, see, he stirs, new knowledge fires his brain,
And Cupid's vision bids him wake again.
Dione's Daughter! but how fair he is,   110
Would it be wrong to rouse him with a kiss?

(She stoops down and kisses him, then withdraws
into the shadow.)

Pierrot (Rubbing his eyes).
    Celestial messenger! remain, remain;
Or, if a vision, visit me again!
What is this light, and whither am I come
To sleep beneath the stars so far from home?

(Rises slowly to his feet.)

Pierrot.
    Stay, I remember this is Venus' Grove,
And I am hither come to encounter——

The Lady (Coming forward, but veiled).
                        Love!

Pierrot (In ecstasy, throwing himself at her feet)
    Then have I ventured and encountered Love?

The Lady.
    Not yet, rash boy! and, if thou wouldst be wise,   120
Return unknowing; he is safe who flies.

Pierrot.

> Never, sweet lady, will I leave this place
> Until I see the wonder of thy face.
> Goddess or Naiad! lady of this Grove,
> Made mortal for a night to teach me love,
> Unveil thyself, although thy beauty be
> Too luminous for my mortality.

The Lady (Unveiling).

> Then, foolish boy, receive at length thy will:
> Now knowest thou the greatness of thine ill.

Pierrot.

> Now have I lost my heart, and gained my goal.   130

The Lady.

> Didst thou not read the warning on the scroll?

Pierrot (Picking up the parchment).

> I read it all, as on this quest I fared,
> Save where it was illegible and hard.

The Lady.

> Alack! poor scholar, wast thou never taught
> A little knowledge serveth less than naught?
> Hadst thou perused—but, stay, I will explain
> What was the writing which thou didst disdain.

(Reads)
"*Au Petit Trianon*, at night's full noon,
Mortal, beware the kisses of the moon!
Whoso seeks her she gathers like a flower—   140
He gives a life, and only gains an hour."

Pierrot (Laughing recklessly).

    Bear me away to thine enchanted bower,
All of my life I venture for an hour.

The Lady.

    Take up thy destiny of short delight;
I am thy lady for a summer's night.
Lift up your viols, maidens of my train,
And work such havoc on this mortal's brain
That for a moment he may touch and know
Immortal things, and be full Pierrot.
White music, Nymphs! Violet and Eglantine!   150
To stir his tired veins like magic wine.
What visitants across his spirit glance,
Lying on lilies, while he watch me dance?
Watch, and forget all weary things of earth,
All memories and cares, all joy and mirth,
While my dance woos him, light and rhythmical,
And weaves his heart into my coronal.
Music, more music for his soul's delight:
Love is his lady for a summer's night.

(Pierrot reclines, and gazes at her while she dances.
The dance finished, she beckons to him: he rises
dreamily, and stands at her side.)

Pierrot.

> Whence came, dear Queen, such magic melody?　160

The Lady.

> Pan made it long ago in Arcady.

Pierrot.

> I heard it long ago, I know not where,
> As I knew thee, or ever I came here.
> But I forgot all things—my name and race,
> All that I ever knew except thy face.
> Who art thou, lady?　Breathe a name to me,
> That I may tell it like a rosary.
> Thou, whom I sought, dear Dryad of the trees,
> How art thou designate—art thou Heart's-Ease?

The Lady.

> Waste not the night in idle questioning,　170
> Since Love departs at dawn's awakening.

Pierrot.

> Nay, thou art right; what recks thy name or state,
> Since thou art lovely and compassionate.
> Play out thy will on me: I am thy lyre.

The Lady.

> I am to each the face of his desire.

Pierrot.

　　I am not Pierrot, but Venus' dove,
　　Who craves a refuge on the breast of love.

The Lady.

　　What wouldst thou of the maiden of the moon?
　　Until the cock crow I may grant thy boon.

Pierrot.

　　Then, sweet Moon Maiden, in some magic car,　　180
　　Wrought wondrously of many a homeless star—
　　Such must attend thy journeys through the skies,—
　　Drawn by a team of milk-white butterflies,
　　Whom, with soft voice and music of thy maids,
　　Thou urgest gently through the heavenly glades;
　　Mount me beside thee, bear me far away
　　From the low regions of the solar day;
　　Over the rainbow, up into the moon,
　　Where is thy palace and thine opal throne;
　　There on thy bosom——　　　　　　　　　190

The Lady.　　　　　　　　　Too ambitious boy!
　　I did but promise thee one hour of joy.
　　This tour thou plannest, with a heart so light,
　　Could hardly be completed in a night.
　　Hast thou no craving less remote than this?

Pierrot.

　　Would it be impudent to beg a kiss?

The Lady.

> I say not that: yet prithee have a care!
> Often audacity has proved a snare.
> How wan and pale do moon-kissed roses grow—
> Dost thou not fear my kisses, Pierrot?   200

Pierrot.

> As one who faints upon the Libyan plain
> Fears the oasis which brings life again!

The Lady.

> Where far away green palm trees seem to stand
> May be a mirage of the wreathing sand.

Pierrot.

> Nay, dear enchantress, I consider naught,
> Save mine own ignorance, which would be taught.

The Lady.

> Dost thou persist?

Pierrot.

> I do entreat this boon!

(She bends forward, their lips meet: he withdraws
with a petulant shiver. She utters a peal of clear
laughter.)

The Lady.

> Why art thou pale, fond lover of the moon?

Pierrot.

 Cold are thy lips, more cold than I can tell; 210
Yet would I hang on them, thine icicle!
Cold is thy kiss, more cold than I could dream
Arctus sits, watching the Boreal stream:
But with its frost such sweetness did conspire
That all my veins are filled with running fire;
Never I knew that life contained such bliss
As the divine completeness of a kiss.

The Lady.

 Apt scholar! so love's lesson has been taught,
Warning, as usual, has gone for naught.

Pierrot.

 Had all my schooling been of this soft kind, 220
To play the truant I were less inclined.
Teach me again! I am a sorry dunce--
I never knew a task by conning once.

The Lady.

 Then come with me! below this pleasant shrine
Of Venus we will presently recline,
Until birds' twitter beckon me away
To mine own home, beyond the milky-way.
I will instruct thee, for I deem as yet
Of Love thou knowest but the alphabet.

Pierrot.

> In its sweet grammar I shall grow most wise,   230
> If all its rules be written in thine eyes.

(The lady sits upon a step of the temple, and Pierrot leans upon his elbow at her feet, regarding her.)

Pierrot.

> Sweet contemplation! how my senses yearn
> To be thy scholar always, always learn.
> Hold not so high from me thy radiant mouth,
> Fragrant with all the spices of the South;
> Nor turn, O sweet! thy golden face away,
> For with it goes the light of all my day.
> Let me peruse it, till I know by rote
> Each line of it, like music, note by note;
> Raise thy long lashes, Lady! smile again: 240
> These studies profit me.

(Taking her hand.)

The Lady.   Refrain, refrain!

Pierrot (With passion).

> I am but studious, so do not stir;
> Thou art my star, I thine astronomer!
> Geometry was founded on thy lip.

(Kisses her hand.)

The Lady.

    This attitude becomes not scholarship!
Thy zeal I praise; but, prithee, not so fast,
Nor leave the rudiments until the last.
Science applied is good, but t'were a schism
To study such before the catechism.   250
Bear thee more modestly, while I submit
Some easy problems to confirm thy wit.

Pierrot.

    In all humility my mind I pit
Against her problems which would test my wit.

The Lady (Questioning him from a little book bound
    deliciously in vellum).

      What is Love?
   Is it a folly,
   Is it mirth, or melancholy?
      Joys above,
   Are there many, or not any?
      What is love?   260

Pierrot (Answering in a very humble attitude of
    scholarship).

      If you please,
      A most sweet folly!
   Full of mirth and melancholy:
      Both of these!
   In its sadness worth all gladness,
      If you please!

The Lady.

> Prithee where,
> Goes Love a-hiding?
> Is he long in his abiding
>   Anywhere?   270
> Can you bind him when you find him;
>   Prithee, where?

Pierrot.

> With spring days
> Love comes and dallies:
> Upon the mountains, through the valleys
>   Lie Love's ways.
> Then he leaves you and deceives you
>   In spring days.

The Lady.

> Thine answers please me: 'tis thy turn to ask.
> To meet thy questioning be now my task.   280

Pierrot.

> Since I know thee, dear Immortal,
> Is my heart become a blossom,
> To be worn upon thy bosom.
> When thou turn me from this portal,
> Whither shall I, hapless mortal,
> Seek love out and win again
> Heart of me that thou retain?

The Lady.

> In and out the woods and valleys,
> Circling, soaring like a swallow,
> Love shall flee and thou shalt follow: 290
> Though he stops awhile and dallies,
> Never shalt thou stay his malice!
> Moon-kissed mortals seek in vain
> To possess their hearts again!

Pierrot.

> Tell me, Lady, shall I never
> Rid me of this grievous burden!
> Follow Love and find his guerdon
> In no maiden whatsoever?
> Wilt thou hold my heart for ever?
> Rather would I thine forget,   300
> In some earthly Pierrette!

The Lady.

> Thus thy fate, whate'er thy will is!
> Moon-struck child, go seek my traces
> Vainly in all mortal faces!
> In and out among the lilies,
> Court each rural Amaryllis:
> Seek the signet of Love's hand
> In each courtly Corisande!

Pierrot.

> Now, verily, sweet maid, of school I tire:
> These answers are not such as I desire.   310

The Lady.
    Why art thou sad?

Pierrot.   I dare not tell.

The Lady (Caressingly).   Come, say!

Pierrot.
    Is love all schooling, with no time to play?

The Lady.
    Though all love's lessons be a holiday,
    Yet I will humour thee: what wouldst thou play?

Pierrot.
    What are the games that small moon-maids
        enjoy,
    Or is their time all spent in staid employ?

The Lady.
    Sedate they are, yet games they much enjoy:
    They skip with stars, the rainbow is their toy.   320

Pierrot.
    That is too hard!

The Lady.   For mortal's play.

Pierrot.   What then?

The Lady.
    Teach me some pastime from the world of men.

Pierrot.

    I have it, maiden.

The Lady.   Can it soon be taught?

Pierrot.

    A simple game, I learnt it at the Court.
    I sit by thee.

The Lady.   But, prithee, not so near.

Pierrot.

    That is essential, as will soon appear.   330
    Lay here thine hand, which cold night dews anoint,
    Washing its white——

The Lady.   Now is this to the point?

Pierrot.

    Prithee, forbear! Such is the game's design.

The Lady.

    Here is my hand.

Pierrot.   **I cover it with mine.**

The Lady.

    What must I next?

    (They play.)

Pierrot.   Withdraw.

The Lady.   It goes too fast.

(They continue playing, until Pierrot catches her
hand.)

Pierrot (Laughing).
          Tis done.   I win my forfeit at the last.   340

(He tries to embrace her.   She escapes; he chases
her round the stage; she eludes him.)

The Lady.
          Thou art not quick enough.   Who hopes to catch
A moon-beam, must use twice as much despatch.

Pierrot (Sitting down sulkily).
          I grow aweary, and my heart is sore.
Thou dost not love me; I will play no more.

(He buries his face in his hands: the lady stands
over him.)

The Lady.
          What is this petulance?

Pierrot.   'Tis quick to tell—
          Thou hast but mocked me.

The Lady.   Nay!   I love thee well!

Pierrot.

> Repeat those words, for still within my breast
> A whisper warns me they are said in jest.   350

The Lady.

> I jested not: at daybreak I must go,
> Yet loving thee far better than thou know.

Pierrot.

> Then, by this altar, and this sacred shrine,
> Take my sworn troth, and swear thee wholly mine!
> The gods have wedded mortals long ere this.

The Lady.

> There was enough betrothal in my kiss.
> What need of further oaths?

Pierrot.   That bound not thee!

The Lady.

> Peace! since I tell thee that it may not be.
> But sit beside me whilst I soothe thy bale   360
> With some moon fancy or celestial tale.

Pierrot.

> Tell me of thee, and that dim, happy place
> Where lies thine home, with maidens of thy race!

The Lady (Seating herself).

    Calm is it yonder, very calm; the air
For mortals' breath is too refined and rare;
Hard by a green lagoon our palace rears
Its dome of agate through a myriad years.
A hundred chambers its bright walls enthrone,
Each one carved strangely from a precious stone.
Within the fairest, clad in purity,   370
Our mother dwelleth immemorially:
Moon-calm, moon-pale, with moon stones on her
    gown
The floor she treads with little pearls is sown;
She sits upon a throne of amethysts,
And orders mortal fortunes as she lists;
I, and my sisters, all around her stand,
And, when she speaks, accomplish her demand.

Pierrot.

    Methought grim Clotho and her sisters twain
With shrivelled fingers spun this web of bane!

The Lady.

    Theirs and my mother's realm is far apart;   380
Hers is the lustrous kingdom of the heart,
And dreamers all, and all who sing and love,
Her power acknowledge, and her rule approve.

Pierrot.

    Me, even me, she hath led into this grove.

The Lady.
     Yea, thou art one of hers! But, ere this night,
Often I watched my sisters take their flight
Down heaven's stairway of the clustered stars
To gaze on mortals through their lattice bars;
And some in sleep they woo with dreams of bliss
Too shadowy to tell, and some they kiss.   390
But all to whom they come, my sisters say,
Forthwith forget all joyance of the day,
Forget their laughter and forget their tears,
And dream away with singing all their years—
Moon-lovers always!

(She sighs.)

Pierrot.   Why art sad, sweet Moon?

(Laughing.)

The Lady.
    For this, my story, grant me now a boon.

Pierrot.
    I am thy servitor.

The Lady.   Would, then, I knew
More of the earth, what men and women do.   400

Pierrot.
    I will explain.

The Lady.   Let brevity attend
Thy wit, for night approaches to its end.

Pierrot.

    Once was I a page at Court, so trust in me:
That's the first lesson of society.

The Lady.
    Society?

Pierrot.   I mean the very best
Pardy! thou wouldst not hear about the rest.
I know it not, but am a *petit maître*
At rout and festival and *bal champêtre*.   410
But since example be instruction's ease,
Let's play the thing.—Now, Madame, if you please!

(He helps her to rise, and leads her forward: then
he kisses her hand, bowing over it with a very
courtly air.)

The Lady.
    What am I, then?

Pierrot.   A most divine Marquise!
Perhaps that attitude hath too much ease.

(Passes her.)

Ah, that is better! To complete the plan,
Nothing is necessary save a fan.

The Lady.

    Cool is the night, what needs it?

Pierrot.   Madame, pray

    Reflect, it is essential to our play.   420

The Lady (Taking a lily).

    Here is my fan!

Pierrot.   So, use it with intent:

    The deadliest arm in beauty's armament!

The Lady.

    What do we next?

Pierrot.   We talk!

The Lady.   But what about?

Pierrot.

    We quiz the company and praise the rout;
    Are polished, petulant, malicious, sly,
    Or what you will, so reputations die.
    Observe the Duchess in Venetian lace,   430
    With the red eminence.

The Lady.   A pretty face!

Pierrot.

> For something tarter set thy wits to search—
> "She loves the churchman better than the church."

The Lady.

> Her blush is charming; would it were her own!

Pierrot.

> Madame is merciless!

The Lady.　　　　　　　　　Is that the tone?

Pierrot.

> The very tone: I swear thou lackest naught,
> Madame was evidently bred at Court.

The Lady.

> Thou speakest glibly: 'tis not of thine age.　　　440

Pierrot.

> I listened much, as best becomes a page.

The Lady.

> I like thy Court but little——

Pierrot.　　　　　　　　　Hush! the Queen!

> Bow, but not low—thou knowest what I mean.

The Lady.

> Nay, that I know not!

Pierrot.   Though she wear a crown,
  'Tis from La Pompadour one fears a frown.

The Lady.
    Thou art a child: thy malice is a game.

Pierrot.
    A most sweet pastime—scandal is its name.

The Lady.
    Enough, it wearies me.   450

Pierrot.   Then, rare Marquise,
  Desert the crowd to wander through the trees.

    (He bows low, and she curtsies; they move round
the stage. When they pass before the Statue he
seizes her hand and falls on his knee.)

The Lady.
    What wouldst thou now?

Pierrot.   Ah, prithee, what, save thee!

The Lady.
    Was this included in thy comedy?

Pierrot.
    Ah, mock me not! In vain with quirk and jest
  I strive to quench the passion in my breast;

In vain thy blandishments would make me play:
Still I desire far more than I can say.
My knowledge halts, ah, sweet, be piteous,   460
Instruct me still, while time remains to us,
Be what thou wist, Goddess, moon-maid, *Marquise*,
So that I gather from thy lips heart's ease,
Nay, I implore thee, think thee how time flies!

The Lady.

    Hush! I beseech thee, even now night dies.

Pierrot.

    Night, day, are one to me for thy soft sake.

(He entreats her with imploring gestures, she hesitates: then puts her finger on her lip, hushing him.)

The Lady.

    It is too late, for hark! the birds awake.

Pierrot.

    The birds awake! It is the voice of day!

The Lady.

    Farewell, dear youth! They summon me away.

(The light changes, it grows daylight: and music imitates the twitter of the birds. They stand gazing at the morning: then Pierrot sinks back upon his bed, he covers his face in his hands.)

The Lady (Bending over him).

    Music, my maids! His weary senses steep
In soft untroubled and oblivious sleep,   470
With mandragore anoint his tirèd eyes,
That they may open on mere memories,
Then shall a vision seem his lost delight,
With love, his lady for a summer's night.
Dream thou hast dreamt all this, when thou awake,
Yet still be sorrowful, for a dream's sake.
I leave thee, sleeper! Yea, I leave thee now,
Yet take my legacy upon thy brow:
Remember me, who was compassionate,
And opened for thee once, the ivory gate.   480
I come no more, thou shalt not see my face
When I am gone to mine exalted place:
Yet all thy days are mine, dreamer of dreams,
All silvered over with the moon's pale beams:
Go forth and seek in each fair face in vain,
To find the image of thy love again.
All maids are kind to thee, yet never one
Shall hold thy truant heart till day be done.
Whom once the moon has kissed, loves long and
      late,
Yet never finds the maid to be his mate.   490
Farewell, dear sleeper, follow out thy fate.

(The Moon Maiden withdraws: a song is sung from
behind: it is full day.)

The Moon Maiden's Song

Sleep! Cast thy canopy
　　Over this sleeper's brain,
Dim grow his memory,
　　When he awake again.

Love stays a summer night,
　　Till lights of morning come;
Then takes her wingèd flight
　　Back to her starry home.

Sleep! Yet thy days are mine;　　　500
　　Love's seal is over thee:
Far though my ways from thine,
　　Dim though thy memory.

Love stays a summer night,
　　Till lights of morning come;
Then takes her wingèd flight
　　Back to her starry home.

(When the song is finished, the curtain falls upon
Pierrot sleeping.)

The End

APPENDIXES

APPENDIX I

EPILOGUE TO

THE PIERROT
OF THE MINUTE

BY WILLIAM THEODORE PETERS

(Spoken in the character of Pierrot)

The sun is up, yet ere a body stirs,
A word with you, sweet ladies and dear sirs,
(Although on no account let any say
That *Pierrot* finished Mr. Dowson's play.)

One night, not long ago, at Baden-Baden,—
The birthday of the Duke,—his pleasure garden
Was lighted gaily with *feu d'artifice*,
With candles, rockets, and a centre-piece
Above the conversation house, on high,
Outlined in living fire against the sky,
A glittering *Pierrot*, radiant, white,
Whose heart beat fast, who danced with sheer delight,
Whose eyes were blue, whose lips were rosy red,
Whose *pompons* too were fire, while on his head
He wore a little cap, and I am told
That rockets covered him with showers of gold.
"That our applause, you well deserve to win it,"
They cried: "Bravo! the *Pierrot* of the minute!"

What with applause and gold, one must confess
That *Pierrot* had "arrived", achieved success,
When, as it happened, presently, alas!
A terrible disaster came to pass.
His nose grew dim, the people gave a shout,
His red lips paled, both his blue eyes went out.
There rose a sullen sound of discontent,
The golden shower of rockets was all spent;
He left off dancing with a sudden jerk,
For he was nothing but a firework.
The garden darkened and the people in it
Cried, "He is dead,—the *Pierrot* of the minute!"

With every artist it is even so;
The artist, after all, is a *Pierrot*—
A *Pierrot* of the minute, *naif*, clever,
But art is back of him, She lives for ever!

Then pardon my Moon Maid and me, because
We craved the golden shower of your applause!
Pray shrive us both for having tried to win it,
And cry, "Bravo!   The *Pierrot* of the minute!"

APPENDIX II

ANALYSIS OF
MANUSCRIPT BOOK

PAGE	TITLE	REMARKS	DATE
Front end paper	To Cynara		
There is no p. 1			
2	A Mosaic		
3	Hymn to Aphrodite	*Decorations*	
4	Requiem		
5	Potnia Thea		Aug. 1886
7	Rondeau		
8	Rondeau		
9	Sonnets I. n Memoriam H. C. *ob.* Feb. 24, 1886		
10	Sonnets II. Novalis		
11	Sonnets of a Little Girl I		
12	Sonnets of a Little Girl II		
13	Sonnets of a Little Girl III		
14	Sonnets of a Little Girl IV	*London Society,* Nov. 1886	1885
15	Sonnets of a Little Girl V		
15	Sonnets of a Little Girl VI		
16	Sonnets of a Little Girl VII		
17	Sonnets of a Little Girl VIII. Epilogue	*Decorations*	
18	La Jeunesse n'a qu'un temps		
19	Song of the XIXth Century		
19	A Lullaby		
29	Spleen	This is deleted *in toto*	

PAGE	TITLE	REMARKS	DATE
21	Spleen		
22	After Many Years		
24	Praeterita		
(26, 27, 28 missing)			
29	Adios		
29	A Song for Spring Time	*Decorations*	
30	Seraphita—Seraphitus		
(bottom half of 31 cut away)			
32	Sonnet. April	*Temple Bar,* April 1889. *Verses.* Title enlarged to "My Lady April"	April 1888
33	It is Finished		
34	Ere I Go Hence		
35	Transit Gloria		May 19, 1887
38	Sonnet. To Nature		Aug. 1887
39	Awakening		May 1888
40	Lullaby		May 1888
42	The Old Year		Dec. 31, 1888
44	The New Year		Jan. 1889
48	From the Icelandic		April 1889
49a	This is the Wisdom of the Wise	*Decorations* as "Wisdom"	
49	Love's Epilogue		Aug. 2, 1889
51	To Hélène, a Rondeau	*Temple Bar,* Sept. 1893, as "A Roundel". *Decorations* as "Beyond"	Aug. 1889
52	Rondeau. Hélène		Aug. 1889
53	Rondeau. Jadis!	*Decorations* as "Jadis"	Aug. 24, 1889
54	Roundel. To Hélène		Oct. 27, 1889
55	To His Mistress	*Decorations*	Dec. 2, 1889
56	Rondel		Feb. 4, 1890
(57, 58 missing)			

PAGE	TITLE	REMARKS	DATE
77	Carthusians	*Decorations* May 27, 1891	
79	Claire : la lune !	*Century Guild* July 20, *Hobby Horse,* 1891 1891, *Verses*	
80	From the French of Paul Verlaine, "Il pleut douce- ment . . ."	z*Decorations* Sept. 8, 1891	
(81, 82 missing)			
83	Ah, dans ces mornes séjours les jamais sont les toujours	*Rhymers' Club II,* Sept. 13, 1894, Verses 1891	
85	Against my Lady Burton	Nov. 10, 1891	
86	Vain Resolves	*Verses* Dec. 3, 1891	
Back cover	Marguerite. A Villanelle	*Temple Bar,* Dec. 31, May 1894. 1891 *Verses*	
Loose half- sheet (from same book)	Adios !	*London Society,* March 1887	

*	1 loose sheet, 7	1 stanza from Sapientiae Lunae	*Verses* Feb. 19, 1892
	1 loose sheet, 8a reverse of above	After Paul Verlaine, Spleen	*Decorations* Feb. 1892

* from another book

grey paper p. 1b	1 stanza from To a Lady Asking Foolish Questions (*Decorations*)	"fragments, to be worked up"
grey paper 12-14	De Amore	

NOTES

NOTES

Note.   Words enclosed between brackets [ ] have been struck out by the Poet.   Another version appears above in each case.

On seven occasions BM. Add. MS. 45135 is referred to. This is an exercise book into which Sam Smith pasted the seven autograph MSS. which Dowson gave him; the volume was bequeathed to the British Museum on the owner's death in 1938.

VERSES

Verses, which was Dowson's first book of poems, appeared in 1896.   The British Museum date of receipt is 24 July 1896. The edition consisted of 300 copies on hand-made paper and 30 large-paper copies on Japanese vellum, printed by the Chiswick Press.   It was not reprinted in Dowson's lifetime: Mr. Arthur Symons' collected edition (Lane, 1905) is reprinted from the first with a few misprints and the dedications omitted.

The practice of dedicating each poem in a book separately was imitated from Verlaine, who did so in Amour (1888), Dédicaces (1890) and Invectives (1896).   (In the preface to Dédicaces Verlaine wrote: "ces quelques ballades et sonnets sont tout intimes et ne visent que quelques amis et bons camarades de l'auteur qui les leur dédie exclusivement, sans autre intention que leur plaire."   Several of Dowson's contemporaries subscribed to the practice, notably his friend John Gray, in his Silverpoints (1893).   In reviewing Verses, The Times referred to it: "Mr. Ernest Dowson labels each of the short pieces that make up his Verses as having been written specially for a particular person. Of this curious practice Beata Solitudo.   For Sam Smith may be cited as a pleasing example.   It may be rather alarming, however, for the friends of those mentioned to come across such a heading to a page as Extreme Unction.   For Lionel Johnson or A Requiem.   For John Gray when there is no reason to believe that the gentlemen in question are anything but alive and well."

The cover was designed by Aubrey Beardsley.

Page 32.   Vitae summa brevis spem nos vetat incohare longam

This poem appears in print for the first time in Verses. *No MS. version is known to me.*

Vitae summa brevis . . . longam: *Horace, Odes I, 4, 15.* "*How should a mortal's hopes be long, when short his being's date.*" (*Conington's version.*)

Page 33.   In Preface: for Adelaide

Adelaide: *Adelaide Faltinowicz, the best-known object of Dowson's unhappy affections.*

Page 34.   A Coronal

This poem appeared in print for the first time in Verses. *Two MS. versions of it are known: one in F (p. 64), and the second in a letter to Victor Plarr (referred to as P). The latter was written about 5 March, 1891 when Dowson and Plarr were discussing the possibility of publishing a book of verse together under the title of* Vine Leaf and Violet. *This* Coronal *was to be the opening poem.*

Title.   *P: none.   F:* A Dedication: with His poems and Her Days to His Lady; and to Love.

Against the poem in F is a note: Rejected: Longmans Mag. *At the end it is dated:* Oct. 16th. 90.

1. vine,) *P:* Vine, 2. frail, fair wreath) *P:* frail fair wreath,
   3. entwine:) *F, P:* entwine!

5. Fragrant) *F:* Fragrant / Perfumed *no choice made.   P:* Perfumed
   6. divine) *F:* divine, 7. day) *F:* day,   night) *F:* Eve *P:* eve *corrected to* night   near.) *F, P:* near:
   8. vine) *F:* vine, 9. entwine.) *F, P:* entwine! 10. vine) *F:* vine, *P:* Vine 12. entwine.) *F, P:* entwine! 14. falls,) *F, P:* falls

15. blossoms,) *P:* flowers of *corrected to* blossoms;   mine,) *F, P:* mine 16. head.) *F:* head: *P:* head! 18. entwine.) *F:* entwine! 20. Love) *P:* Love,   dies) *P:* dies, 21. entwine.) *F, P:* entwine!

23. Over) *P:* Upon *corrected to* Over   pale, cold eyes) *F:* cold, pale eyes *P:* cold pale eyes
    24. Proserpine,) *P:* Proserpine

25. At set of sun we lay) *F:* At fall of night we *deleted,* we sorrowfully lay *deleted, and the final version inserted. P is the same. It is curious that Dowson should have experienced so much trouble over this line, and the same trouble in each MS. version.*

    26. Vine) *P:* vine, 27. entwine.) *F:* entwine!

Page 36. Nuns of the Perpetual Adoration

This poem appeared for the fourth time in Verses. *It was first printed in the* Century Guild Hobby Horse, *Vol. VI, 1891, p. 136 (HH); where three poems, this,* Flos Lunae, *and* Amor Umbratilis, *were grouped together under the title* In Praise of Solitude. *Next M. Davray printed it in the* Mercure de France, *March 1892, with a French translation opposite (MF). Its third appearance formed part of Dowson's contribution to the* First Book of the Rhymers' *Club, 1892, p. 10 (RC). Lionel Johnson's copy of the Rhymers' Club Book exists, in which "in several places Johnson has written in later corrections made by Dowson to his poems" (Elkin Mathews, London; catalogue 42, A. J. A. Symons Collection, item 372); this is referred to as RCa. There are also three MS. versions: one in F, p. 72, the second a single leaf in the Collection of Mr. Michael Holland (MH), and the third a single leaf at Queen's College, Oxford (O). It was submitted to Herbert Horne in a letter dated 4 Sept. '91.*

The Poem is dated at the end of the F and O versions: Feb. 10. 1891

Title. *F, MH:* Ursulines of the Perpetual Adoration
    O: Nuns, *etc. corrected to* Ursulines, *etc.*
    HH: The Carmelite Nuns of the Perpetual Adoration
    MF, RC: Carmelite Nuns of the Perpetual Adoration

    1. secure;) *F, MH, O, HH:* secure, walls,) *MH, MF, RC:* walls; 2. lamp,) *F, O, HH:* lamp; *MF:* lamps, pray:) *MF:* pray; 3. them) *F, MH, O, HH, MF, RC:* them, falls,) *O, MF, RC:* falls; 4. them) *F, MH, HH, MF, RC:* them,

5. These heed not time;) *F:* These smile at time: *MH, O, HH, MF, RC:* time:
    6. rosary,) *F, MH, O, HH, MF, RC:* rosary;

7. *F:* Where on their $\frac{\text{hours}}{\text{lives}}$ are $\frac{\text{threaded,}}{\text{woven,}}$ for Christ's sake; threaded) *O:* woven,
    7. lives) *HH, RCa:* hours   threaded) *HH:* threaded,
    8. Meekness) *HH:* Meekness,   vigilance) *HH:* vigilance,   10. Life-long) *HH, MF:* Life long   11. penances) *F, MH, O, MF, RC:* penances,

12. Are) *F: is deleted, are added in pencil.*   Are fragrant incense) *O:* $\frac{\text{Is fragrant incense [mount]}}{\text{[Like incense afloat up]}}$ Sacrificed.) *MH, O:* sacrifict.
    13. Outside,) *F, O:* Outside   wild) *F:* wild,   passionate;) *O:* passionate:

14. Man's weary laughter) *F: the sound of laughter corrected in pencil to same.*
    14. laughter) *MH, O, RC:* laughter,

14. his sick despair) *F: of wild despair corrected in pencil to same. O:* of loud despair
    14. despair) *HH:* despair,   15, Entreat at their) *MH, O:* Entreateth their

17–20. *F: a complete previous version of this stanza appears and is deleted in favour of the final version, which is added, first in pencil and then inked over, on the opposite page. It reads:*

The roses of the world, they knew, $\frac{\text{saw}}{\text{[shall]}}$ fade,
And be trod under by the hurrying feet:
They saw the $\frac{\text{pageant}}{\text{glory}}$ of the world displayed;
They saw the bitter did outweigh the sweet.

O has this version intact, with the following small variations:
    1. saw) *O:* should   3. pageant) *O:* glory
    17. displayed;) *MH, MF, RC:* displayed,   18. of it,) *MH:* there of *corrected*   sweet;) *F, MH, HH, MF, RC:* sweet: 21. Therefore) *HH:* Therefore,   desire,) *O:*

desire 22. hands) *HH:* hands, sanctuary;) *F:* sanc-
tuary, *O, HH:* sanctuary: *MF, RC:* Sanctuary; 23.
veiled) *F, MH, HH:* vailed heads) *MH, HH:* heads,
attire:) *O:* attire, *HH:* attire; 24. vanity.) *F:*
Vanity. 26. the) *RCa:* that 27. sweet) *RCa:* dear
Star) *HH:* star dispels . . . night) *F:* shines on them
through the night, *corrected. O: the same as F, intact.*

28. The . . . humanity.) *F:* And lightens them in lone
security. *corrected O: as F, but intact.*

29. secure;) *RC:* serene; mild:) *F, O:* mild, *HH:*
mild;

30. choice) *F:* part *corrected O:* choice *corrected to* part
best?) *F, O, HH:* best:

31. Yea!) *F:* Yea *O:* so soon *corrected RCa:* Ah!
fade,) *F, HH:* fade; wild;) *O:* wild, 32. there,)
O, HH: there beside) *F:* beneath *corrected O:* beneath
there,) *HH:* there rest.) *F:* rest!

Page 38. Villanelle of Sunset

This poem was first printed in the Book of the Rhymers' Club,
*1892, p. 83. There is also a MS. version in F, p. 62. It was
divided into stanzas for the first time in* Verses. *At the end of F
the poem is dated:* June 2/1890.

Title. *F:* Villanelle
1. Child!) *F, RC:* child rest) *F:* rest, 2. day,)
F: day:—
5. play) *F:* play— 6. child!) *F:* child *RC:* child!
rest.) *F:* rest!

7. My white bird,) *F:* My robin *corrected*
8. lay:) *F:* lay— 10. confest) *F:* confess't 11. slum-
ber:) *F:* slumber:— they!) *F:* they— 12. Child!
and rest) *F:* child & rest! *RC:* child! 13. manifest,)
F: manifest 14. way:) *F:* way— 16. flower!) *F:*
flower, breast,) *F:* breast 17. thee) *RC:* thee,
alway:) *F:* alway. 18. child! and rest;) *F:* child and
rest, *RC:* child!

19. Behold) Verses *prints a comma after* Behold, *but as the line occurs elsewhere in the poem three times without any comma, and the F MS, has none, I have taken it to be a misprint and corrected it. There is no reason why the rhythm of this line should suddenly be changed.*
West!) *F:* West.

Page 39. My Lady April

This poem was first published in Temple Bar, *Vol. LXXXV, part* 341, *April*, 1889, *p.* 514. *It was the first poem of Dowson's which* Temple Bar *accepted. There is also a MS. version in F, p.* 32. *In* Verses *there was a break between the octave and sestet, but this is not supported by the MS., in which the poem is definitely referred to as a sonnet: it is therefore printed here in the more usual sonnet form.*

Title. *F:* Sonnet/ April

Dated at the end in F: April. 1888. *With the additional note:* published Temple Bar 1889.

Dedication. Léopold Nelken was a Pole studying medicine in Paris with whom Dowson became friendly when alone there during the winter of 1895-6.

    1. hair;) *F:* hair *TB:* hair,

2. Twin) *F:* And *corrected* for) *F:* in *corrected* eyes;)
F, TB: eyes, behold) *F:* I see *corrected* pass,) *F:* pass

3. brushing) *F, TB:* crushing
    3. young,) *F:* young 4. high,) *F:* high 5. sweetness:) *F:* sweetness:— fair,) *F:* fair

6. flower-like) *F:* fresh young *TB:* fresh, young beauty,) *F:* beauty

7.) *F:* Mirrors $\frac{out}{[up]}$ love and hope, $\frac{but}{[yet]}$ still, alas,
    7. love:) *TB:* love, alas!) *TB:* alas,

8.) *F: this line was originally written:* Of tears her drooping lashes are not bare. *Corrections forming the printed version were pencilled over the top, but no final decision was made.*
    10. foresee) *F:* foresee, 11. Across) *F:* Athwart

youth) *TB:* youth, 12. days) *F:* months be:)
F: be.— *TB:* be,— 14. barrenness.) *F, TB:* barren-
ness?

Page 40. To One in Bedlam

This poem appeared in print for the third time in Verses. *It was
first published in the* Albemarle, *edited by Hubert Crackanthorpe,
Vol. II, No. 2, August 1892; secondly it formed part of Dowson's
contribution to the* Second Book of the Rhymers' Club (RC2).
No MS. version is known to me.

Dedication. *M. Henry Davray was at that time a great personal
friend of Dowson. He was on the* Mercure de France *and was
charged with reviewing English books. The Rhymers' Club
and the English writers of the 'Nineties as a whole owe their
introduction to French readers to his good offices. M. Davray's
service to French and English literature has been long and
honourable and continued with undiminished vigour until recently.
Among others, Arnold Bennett had considerable occasion to
remember his kindness and enthusiasm, vide his* Journals, *Vol. I,
passim.*

*When translating some of Dowson's poems for publication in
the* Mercure de France, *M Davray chose this as one of them.
He inquired of Dowson the meaning of a few phrases that were
obscure to him, such as "posies" and "scentless wisps of straw",
and in an undated letter from Pont Aven the poet replied, giving
their French equivalent. M. Davray's version does not seem to
have appeared.*

7. enchaunted) *RC2:* enchanted *The "ye olde" form
is so unnecessary here that it is a sore temptation to adopt the
Rhymers' Club emendation; its appearance in one more
authoritative text would certainly induce me to do so.* 8.
stars?) *RC2:* stars'?

13. moon-kissed) *an expression which Dowson used several
times and always with the same inference, cf.* Pierrot of the
Minute 139: Mortal, beware the kisses of the moon!,
293–4: Moon-kissed mortals seek in vain To possess their
hearts again!, *and* 489–90: Whom once the moon has

kissed, loves long and late, Yet never finds the maid to be his mate.

Page 41. Ad Domnulam Suam

This poem was first printed in the Book of the Rhymers' Club, *1892, p. 53 ; there are also two MS. versions: one in F, p. 66 ; the other in a letter [19 Oct, '90.] to Arthur Moore. Of these, the latter is probably the earlier. It is noticeable that the few alterations in the MSS. tend to make the poem more impersonal.*

Title.   *F:* Ad Domnul $\begin{smallmatrix} \text{am Suam} \\ \text{[ae meae]} \end{smallmatrix}$

    M: Ad Domnulam Meam

Dated at the end of F: Oct. 18. 1890.

    1. heart)   *F, M:* heart,   3. part,)   *M:* part

4. this)   *F:* my *corrected*

     5. Child!)   *F, M:* Child,   too)   *M:* so   well,)   *F:* well

6.)   *M:* I can only leave thee

    8. tale,)   *F, M:* tale   9. heart!)   *F:* heart,   *M:* heart

    10. longer,)   *M:* longer   11. part,)   *F, M:* part

13. Soon thou leavest)   *M:* Thou art leaving *corrected*

    13. land;)   *F, M:* land,   14. tresses:)   *F, M:* tresses;

    15. hand;)   *F, M:* hand,   17. heart!)   *F:* heart,   *M:* heart   19. part,)   *F:* part then, we will part,   *M:* then we will part   20. this)   *F:* my *corrected*

Page 42. Amor Umbratilis

This poem was printed for the third time in Verses. *Its first appearance was in the* Century Guild Hobby Horse, *Vol. VI, 1891, p. 137 (HH), see* Nuns of the Perpetual Adoration, *note, p. 245 ; secondly, it was printed in the* Book of the Rhymers' Club, *1892, p. 41. There are also three MS. versions extant: one in F, p. 63 ; a second on the back of a money-lender's letter, dated* October 7, 1890 (O'C). *This letter is now in the possession of Mr. J. Harlin O'Connell. The third is contained in a letter, [16/17 Sept, '90.], to Mr. Arthur Moore. None of these MS. versions is the original draft, the date of composition being given in*

F as a month previous (see post). All are fair copies; the first copied into F, as was Dowson's custom, when the poem was in reasonable shape; the other two written out for a special purpose. The date of acceptance by the Hobby Horse *is given in F (see post) as October 10, so that Dowson must have met Herbert Horne three days previously and copied this exquisite poem out, for submission to him, on the first piece of paper that come to hand: a money-lender's letter.* Title. *F: added in pencil.* Umbratilis—retiring; cf.

> I will keep my soul in a place out of sight,
> Far off, where the pulse of it is not heard.
>
> Swinburne, The Triumph of Time.

M: no title

Dated at the end in F: Sept. 16th 1890. *Opposite the date is pencilled:*

> [*Rejected*] "English Illustrated"
> Accepted "Century Guild Hobby Horse"
> Oct 10th 1890

> Pub C. G. H. H. Oct. 1891
> &
> Book of Rhymers Club, 1892—

Initialled ED *at the end of O'C.*

1. Silence) *F, O'C, M, HH, RC:* silence   sweet!) *O'C, HH, RC:* Sweet! *M:* sweet   2. hear:) *F:* hear *O'C:* hear! *M, HH:* hear,   3. your) *M:* thy *corrected*   feet,) *M:* feet   5. sing,) *O'C, M:* sing   6. heed) *HH:* heed,   7. lilies,) *F, O'C, M:* lilies hands,) *F, O'C, M:* hands   fling) *RC:* fling,

8. Across) *F:* Adown *corrected* *M:* Adown
   10. unmeet) *F:* not meet *corrected*   you!) *F, O'C:* you, *HH:* you; *RC:* you: 11. garland) *RC:* garland,   gathered) *RC:* gathered,   day:) *F, O'C, HH:* day, *M:* day *RC:* day;

12. rosemary and rue) *HH, RC:* rose-mary. *Rosemary for remembrance and rue for sorrow.*

13. You pass) *HH:* you pass,   pass,) *M:* pass 14. cold:) *M:* cold; 15. trodden,) *F, O'C:* trodden

grass,) *F, M:* grass 17. Yea,) *O'C:* Yea cast) *M:*
give *corrected* sweet!) *F:* Sweet,— *O'C, HH, RC:*
Sweet! 18. This) *F:* The *corrected* *M:* The gift,)
F, O'C, HH: gift take:) *F, O'C, M:* take— *HH:*
take,

19. ointment,) *O'C, HH:* ointment feet) *O'C:* sake
corrected *M, HH, RC:* feet,
  20. silence,) *M, O'C:* silence

Page 43. Amor Profanus
This poem appeared for the first time in Verses. *No MS. version
is known.*
Dedication. *Gabriel Lautrec was a Parisian journalist known as
"prince des humoristes".*
  22–25. *Horace,* Odes, *I, 22. Vide also Herrick,* To Vir-
gins to make Much of Time, *Stanza I:*

> Gather ye rosebuds while ye may,
> Old Time is still a-flying;
> And this same flower that smiles to-day,
> To-morrow will be dying.

Also Theocritus, Idylls, *XXIII, 28, 29 and 31:*

> Καὶ τὸ ῥόδον παλὸν ἐστι, καὶ ὁ χρόνος αὐτὸ μαραίνει
> Καὶ τὸ ἴον καλόν ἐστιν ἐν ἔιαρι, καὶ ταχὺ γηρᾷ
> ⋆   ⋆   ⋆   ⋆   ⋆
> Καὶ κάλλος καλόν ἐστι τὸ παιδικόν, ἀλλ' ὀλίγον ζῇ

> The Day is fair but quickly yields to shades,
> The Lilly white, but when 'tis pluckt it fades:
> The Violet lovely, but it withers soon,
> Youth's beauty charming, but tis quickly gone:

*Creech's version, which says lily for rose in the second line, but
is otherwise excellent.*

Page 45. Villanelle of Marguerites
This poem was first printed in Temple Bar, *May 1894. Verses
was its second appearance in print. There is a MS. version in F,
p. 87a.*

Title. *F:* Marguerites. A Villanelle (*the latter seems to be an afterthought*)
> *TB:* Of Marguerites (Villanelle)

Dated at the end of F: Dec 31st 91
> *The poem is printed straight through without stanza breaks in F.*
> 1. Little) *F:* little   passionately,) *TB:* passionately—

2. casts the snowy petals) *F:* cast her rosy petals
> 2. air:) *TB:* air; 3. we how) *F:* we, how   fall!)
> *F, TB:* fall? 4. forestall?) *F:* forestall, 5. care,) *RB:*
> care: 6. passionately,) *TB:* passionately— all!) *F:*
> all. 7. if) *F:* , though *TB:* , if 8. years:) *TB:*
> years; fair;) *F, TB:* fair: 9. we) *F:* we, fall!)
> *F:* fall? 10. if) *F:* that *corrected* 11. voice and eyes)
> *TB:* voice, and eyes, 12. passionately,) *F, TB:*
> passionately—

14. Kissed by the daisies) *F:* Sings to the daisies
> 14. daisies) *TB:* daisies, tear:) *TB:* tear; 15. fall!)
> *TB:* fall? 16. go: but) *F:* go, and   go:) *TB:* go;
> shall) *F:* will 17. were,) *F:* were   bear:) *TB:*
> bear. 18. A little,) *TB:* a little, passionately,) *TB:*
> passionately— all!) *F:* all.

Page 46.   Yvonne of Brittany

This poem appeared for the first time in Verses. *No MS. version is known.*

Dedication. *Marmaduke Langdale was the recipient of an inscribed copy of* Verses. *He was an actor in Sir Frank Benson's company, and wrote occasional verse in the manner of Swinburne.*

The poet seems to have drawn upon the same experience in the composition of this poem as served him in the early chapters of Adrian Rome. *There is also a faint suggestion of* The Orchard *by Swinburne. This poem has a beautiful pictorial counterpart in Charles Conder's* Apple Orchard in Brittany *in the Tate Gallery.*

Page 48.   Benedictio Domini
This poem appeared for the first time in Verses.   *No MS. version
is known.*

Dedication.   *Selwyn Image, 1849–1930, artist, writer on art and
    joint editor with Herbert Horne of the* Hobby Horse, *a resusci-
    tation in 1893 of the* Century Guild Hobby Horse *(1886–92).*

Page 49.   Growth.
This poem first appeared in the Second Book of the Rhymers'
Club, *1894, p. 83.   No MS. version of it is known.   There are
no differences between the text in the Rhymers' Club Book and*
Verses, *which is most unusual.   There is also no dedication:
indeed, there could be none, for, almost more than any poem in the
volume,* Growth *bears out Dowson's preface to* Adelaide: To you,
who are my verses, as on some future day, if you ever care to
read them, you will understand. . . .*

Page 50.   Ad Manus Puellae
This poem was printed for the first time in Verses.   *There are two
MS. versions known.   One is contained in a letter to John Gray,
dated February 24, 1893 (G); the second (L) is contained in an
undated letter to John Lane, dated simply* Feb 1893

Title.   G: Manus $\begin{array}{c}\text{Puellae}\\\text{[Dominae]}\end{array}$
        At the top of L is added the quotation:
            Rêves bénis, mains consacrées,
            O ces mains, ses mains vénérées !
                                        Paul Verlaine.

Dedication.   *Leonard Smithers was the publisher of all Dowson's
    books but one,* Dilemmas, *which was placed in the hands of
    Elkin Mathews.   He first became known as a bookseller dealing
    in "curious" works, a business which he continued beside his
    publishing activities.   He commands the highest respect for his
    list, which contained the work of most of the promising young
    authors of the 'Nineties, as well as Beardsley; in addition he
    sponsored* The Savoy.
    1. hands!) *L*: hands,

3.) Charles fut surpris par la blancheur de ses ongles. Ils
étaient brillants, fins du bout, plus nettoyés que les ivoires
de Dieppe, et taillés d'amande—*Flaubert*, Madame Bovary,
Chapter I, 2.
    3. carved) G, L: carved, 4. wrist;) G, L: wrist,
    6. *fleur-de-lys*) G, L: fleur-de-lys,

6.) Since I was tangled in thy beauty's web,
And snared by the ungloving of thy hand.—*Keats*, Sonnet
—to a Lady seen for a few moments at Vauxhall; *the whole
Sonnet bears some relation to Dowson's poem.*
    7. glove;) *L:* glove, 8. odours passing ambergris:)
    G: odours, passing ambergris; *L:* ambergris; 9. love:
    — *L:* love, 10. your) G, L: *your* enough?) *L:*
    enough! 11. pallor) G: pallour ivories;) *L:* ivories,
    12. sea-shell:) G: sea shell; L: sea shell: 13. treasure,)
    G, L: treasure

14. gold, and spice) G: gold or spice
    16. finger-tips) G: finger tips   18. lips:) G: lips!

19.) G: I am always in prison to their commands—
    20. girl,) G: girl   your) *L: your*

Page 51. Flos Lunae

This poem was first printed in the Century Guild Hobby Horse,
Vol. VI, 1891, p. 136 (see Nuns of the Perpetual Adoration,
note, p. 237). *There are three MS. versions known to me: one in
F, p. 79, the second in a letter to Arthur Moore (M) [20 Jul, '91.],
and the third in BM. Add. MS. 45135. (SS.)*

Title. *F:* Claire: la lune!
    M, HH, SS: Fleur de la lune

Dated in both these MS. versions: June 20th 1891, *with* Century
Guild Hobby Horse *added in F.*
    2. speech) *F, M, HH:* speech, 3. surprise.) *F, M,
    HH, SS:* surprise: 4. thee) *F:* thee, reach:) *F, M,
    HH, SS:* reach;

5. alter) *M, SS:* trouble *corrected* eyes!) *M, HH:* eyes.
    6. eyes;) *F, M, HH, SS:* eyes, 8. Though all my life)

SS: Although my life   down and)   *HH:* down, and
   9. sleep,) *HH:* sleep;   12. thee) *F, M, HH, SS:*
thee,   13. prayers) *M, HH:* prayers,   incense) *HH:*
incense,   rise,) *F, M, SS:* rise: *HH:* rise;

14.) *F:* Maid O maid / [Pale daughter] of the lunar night, *M:* Pale daugh-
ter of the lunar night *HH: ditto* night! *SS: ditto* night,
   15. eyes) *M:* eyes!   18. glance) *HH:* glance,

Page 52.   Non sum qualis eram bonae sub regno Cynarae

*This poem, which has won more fame for its author than any other
of his compositions, was printed for the first time in the* Century
Guild Hobby Horse, *Vol. VI, 1891, p. 67. Its next appearance
was in the* Second Book of the Rhymers' Club, 1894, p. 60.
*There are two MS. versions: one in F, p. 70; the second in a
letter [7 Feb, '91.] to Arthur Moore. The latter does not contain the
last stanza.*

Title.   *F, M:* . . . Cynarae! *Horace,* Odes, *IV, I, 3.*
Dated at the end of F: Feb 7, 1891 *with the added note:* Hobby
   Horse April 1891
   1. mine) *F, M, HH:* mine,

3. soul) *F, M, HH, RC2:* soul,   kisses) *F:* roses *corrected*
   wine;) *F:* wine, *HH:* wine:
   4. desolate) *M, HH:* desolate,   passion,) *HH:* passion:
   5. Yea,) *RC2, HH:* Yea!   was) *F:* grew *corrected*
HH, RC2: grew   desolate) *HH:* desolate, *RC2:*
desolate;

6. Cynara! in my fashion.) *F:* Cynara, [after]^in my fashion
   6. Cynara!) *M:* Cynara,   7. night) *M, HH:* night,
      mine heart) *F, RC2:* my breast *M:* my breast,
   HH: my heart,   beat,) *HH, RC2:* beat;   8. Night-
long) *HH:* Night long,   arms) *HH:* arms,   lay;)
HH, RC2: lay: 9. bought) *M, HH, RC2:* bought,
sweet;) *F, HH, RC2:* sweet?   10. desolate) *HH:*
desolate,   11. awoke) *F, M, HH, RC2:* awoke,
found) *HH:* found,   12. Cynara! in my fashion.) *F:*

Cynara, in my fashion! *M:* Cynara,   13. Cynara!)
F, M: Cynara,   wind,) *HH:* wind! *RC2:* wind;
14. riotously) *M:* riotously,   throng,) *HH, RC2:*
throng;

15. Dancing,) *F, RC2:* Dancing   pale, lost) *M: so written,*
but marked for inversion.   mind;) *F:* mind *M:* mind,
HH: mind:
  16. desolate) *HH, RC2:* desolate,   passion,) *F:*
passion *HH:* passion;

17. Yea, all the time,) *F:* Yea desolate *M:* Yea, desolate,
HH: Yea, desolate! *RC2:* Yea! all the time 17. long:)
RC2: long!
  18. Cynara! in my fashion.) *F:* Cynara, in my fashion!
M: Cynara,   19. music) *HH, RC2:* music,   wine,)
HH: wine: *RC2:* wine;   20. But) *HH:* But,

20. When the feast is finished) *F:* when the cups are empty
corrected in pencil; a further suggestion is pencilled on the
opposite page: But when the viols are silent
  20. finished) *HH, RC2:* finished,   21. Cynara!) *F:*
Cynara: thine;) *F, HH:* thine! 22. desolate) *HH:*
desolate,   passion,) *HH:* passion: 23. Yea,) *the*
omission of a comma after Yea *in* Verses *is an obvious mis-*
print. *F:* Yea *HH, RC2:* Yea!   desire:) *F:* desire.
RC2: desire:—   24. Cynara! in my fashion.) *F:*
Cynara, in my fashion!

Page 53. Vanitas

This poem was printed for the second time in Verses, *its previous*
appearance being in the First Book of the Rhymers' Club, 1892,
p. 69. There is a MS. version in F, p. 74.
Dated at the end of F: March 19.91

Opposite is pencilled a note: "On my eyelids is the shadow of
death" Job xvi. 16

The whole verse reads: My face is foul with weeping, and on
my eyelids is the shadow of death.

Dedication. *Mr. Vincent O'Sullivan issued a volume of poems with Elkin Mathews in the same year as* Verses; *he followed Dowson's example in preferring Smithers for his later book. Mr. Holbrook Jackson* (The Eighteen Nineties) *refers to him as at that time " a modern of the moderns".*

1. weeping,) *F:* weeping;   4. dim) *F:* dim, 8. Death,) *F:* Death 9. ways:) *F:* ways! 10. now,) *F:* now 11. crown) *F:* crown, token:) *F:* token, 17. hands:) *RC:* hands;

Bays, palm and laurel were all Roman signs of triumph; cypress was a Roman funeral emblem, and was dedicated to Pluto. This poem has a very great deal in common with Swinburne's Garden of Proserpine, *which, from the influence it had on him, seems to have been a favourite poem of Dowson's. First, the metre is the same, although the stanza-form differs. Secondly, the same sentiments are expressed; and thirdly there are a number of verbal echoes, cf. the first stanza of each, and:*

I am tired of tears and laughter,
And men that laugh and weep   Proserpine, *II,* 1–2
Beyond the need of weeping,   Vanitas, *I,* 1

That even the weariest river
Winds somewhere safe to sea   Proserpine, *XI,* 7–8

Yet, crossed that weary river,
In some ulterior land   Vanitas, *V,* 1–2

19. her) *F:* those *corrected*
20. Haply she) *F:* Ah, she who *corrected*
22. land,) *F:* land   23. ever,) *F:* never   24. hand?) *F:* hand,

Page 55.   Exile

This poem appeared in print for the first time in Verses; *there is a MS. version in BM. Add. MS.* 45135. (SS.)
Dated in SS. 9 May 1892, *at which time Dowson says he had not yet found a title for the poem.*

Dedication.   *Mr. Conal Holmes O'Connell O'Riordan was born in Dublin in* 1874. *He went on the stage at* 17, *and at* 18 *played Engstrand to Lewis Waller's Alving in Ibsen's* Ghosts.

His first book, In the Green Park, *appeared in* 1894, *and he continued to use the pseudonym of Norreys Conell, which he then adopted, until* 1920. *In* 1909 *Mr. O'Riordan succeeded J. M. Synge as Director of the Abbey Theatre, Dublin.*

1. separation) *SS:* separation, 3. imitation) *SS:* imitation, 4. old) *SS:* old, 5. music) *SS:* music, consolation,) *SS:* consolation; 6. me;) *SS:* me: 9. separation) *SS:* separation, 10. hear) *SS:* hear, place) *SS:* place, 12. Your) *SS:* Thy *corrected* face.) *SS:* face! 13. *SS:* You may be dead, and no proclamation 16. for ever) *SS:* , for ever, 17. desolation;) *SS:* desolation,

Page 56. Spleen

This poem appeared in print for the first time in Verses; *no MS. version is known to me.*

Dedication. *Arthur Symons, poet and critic, was born in* 1865, *and died* 1945. *He was a friend of Dowson's middle years.*

Both Baudelaire and Verlaine wrote poems under this title: Verlaine's was translated by Dowson in Decorations *(see page* 79), *while Baudelaire introduced four compositions under the same title into* Les Fleurs du Mal. *All are, of course, very similar in outlook, though Baudelaire's are more violent in expression. The reference to the rain beating on the windows all day (5–6) occurs in Baudelaire's fourth composition (Fleurs de Mal, LXXX, 9–10):*

> Quand la pluie étalant ses immenses traînées
> D'une vaste prison imite les barreaux.

There are no other similarities of diction.

Page 57. O Mors!

This poem appeared in print for the first time in the First Book of the Rhymers' Club, 1892, *p.* 30; *it was then reprinted in* Verses. *Four MS. versions are known to me: one in F, p.* 76; *the second a single leaf, that was in Mr. A. J. A. Symons' Collection (Elkin Mathews' catalogue, No.* 202), *(S), a third, a single leaf, in Mr. Arthur Moore's Collection (M), and the fourth in BM. Add. MS.*

45135 *(SS.). Dowson's predilection for colons in this poem is very noticeable.*

The first three MS. versions are dated at the end: April 28.91

Title. *Vulgate,* Ecclesiasticus XLI, 1.

2. heart!) *SS:* heart:

3.) *F: this is deleted in favour of:* I have no tomorrow
  3. to-morrow) *M:* to morrow, *RC:* to-morrow,

4. We) *F: deleted to:* I   5. Now) *F: deleted to:* So
  7. playing,) *RC:* playing: 8. viol) *F, S:* Viol
  away:) *M:* away!   *SS:* away.   10. Thine) *SS:* Thy
  11. Prithee,) *RC:* Prithee!   playing,) *SS:* playing
  12. gay.) *SS:* gay!   13. spoken;) *F, S:* spoken,
  M, RC, SS: spoken: 14. nothing:) *RC, SS:* nothing;
  16. prevail!) *F, S, M, RC, SS:* prevail: 17. Prithee,)
  RC: Prithee!   18. fail!) *RC:* fail.   19. to-morrow!)
  S, M: to-morrow: *F, RC:* to-morrow,   20. Weep
  nothing:) *SS:* Lay nothing;   nothing:) *S, M:*
  nothing;   only lay) *F:* merely lay   *RC:* merely lay,
  21. In) *RC:* For   sorrow) *F, M, RC:* sorrow,   22.
  way:) *S:* way!   *RC:* way;   23. Let us) *M:* Prithee
  corrected. SS: Prithee

24. This one day!) *RC:* this last day!   *SS:* For one day.

Page 59.   Ah, dans ces mornes séjours
           Les jamais sont les toujours

This poem was first printed in the Second Book of the Rhymers'
Club, 1894, *p.* 120.   *There is a MS. version in F, p.* 83.

Title. *Added in pencil, without Verlaine's name, in F.*

Dated at the end of F: Sept 13th. 1891
  2 *and* 3. dear!) *F:* Dear!   7. bitter,) *F:* bitter   9.
  Nay,) *F:* Nay

11. in truth was I) *F:* ywis, I was *corrected*
  13. tender,) *F:* tender   14. dear!) *F:* Dear!   rare.)
  F: rare   15. them,) *F:* them   17. dear!) *F:* Dear!
  18. death) *F:* Death   you,) *F:* you   18. dear!) *F:*
  Dear!   21. late,) *F:* late   22. part:) *F:* part;

23. mound) *F:* grave   *The strewing of roses on a grave was a Roman custom;*
  25. nay! this is fitter;)   *F:* nay, this is fitter!   26. me;)
  F: me: 27. we who)   *F:* we, who   bitter,)   *F:* bitter

Page 61.   April Love

This poem appeared for the first time in Verses; *no MS. version is known to me.*

Dedication.   *A. C. Hillier was a member of the Rhymers' Club. Dowson collaborated with him in the translation of Muthe's* History of Art.

Page 62.   Vain Hope

This poem appeared for the first time in Verses: *the only MS. version known is in BM. Add. MS.* 45135 (*SS*).

Title.   *SS:* The Gate of Ivory.
  4. day,) *SS:* day! 7. gainsay!) *SS:* gainsay. 10. pains) *SS:* pains; comforted;) *SS:* comforted! 15. Haply,) *SS:* Surely *corrected.* 16. Though late I come,) *SS:* Though I come late, 17. rhyme:) *SS:* rhyme; 18. Her kind, calm eyes) *SS:* Her calm, chaste eyes, 20. know) *SS:* know,   dreams) *SS:* dreams.

Page 63.   Vain Resolves

This poem appeared for the first time in Verses.   *There is a MS. version in F, p.* 86, *at the end of which the poem is dated* Dec 3, 1891.

  3. ancient) *F:* antient 6. desire;) *F:* desire, 7. prayer,) *F:* prayer 8. "I) *F:* I 9. was) *F:* was, 10. singing) *F:* singing, 11. service) *F:* service, 13. were,) *F:* were 14. solitudes) *F:* solitudes,
14. I will fasten me.")   *F:* I pass presently."
  15. passed,)   *F:* stopped, *corrected*
15–16.) *a slight echo of* La Belle Dame Sans Merci
  19. hath) *F:* has 20. eyes!) *F:* eyes.

Page 64.   A Requiem

This poem appeared for the first time in Verses; *no MS. version is known to me.*

Dedication.   *John Gray, who was born in 1866, spent a few years in a Government office, during which period he produced his first book of Verse,* Silverpoints, 1893, *which for its content and its format is one of the outstanding books of the 'Nineties. He then went to the Scots College at Rome, having been a Roman Catholic from boyhood, and his later years were spent at the Church of St. Peter's, Edinburgh, which he built.   He died in 1934.*

1. Neobule) *a beautiful woman to whom Horace addressed the twelfth Ode of his third Book,* Ad Neobulem.   Eam Hebri adolescentis amore captam inertiae se ac desidiae dedisse. *Dowson begins where Horace ends.*

Page 65.   Beata Solitudo

This poem appeared for the first time in Verses; *no MS. version is known to me.*

Dedication.   *Sam Smith was an Oxford friend of Dowson's, who was studying law.   After they had both come down, Dowson saw Smith quite frequently for some years, and the poet gave him seven autograph MSS. of various poems which are now in BM. Add. MS. 45135.   Smith died in 1938.*

23–25.) *cf. Swinburne,* Hymn to Proserpine:
   Ye are Gods, and behold ye shall die . . .
   Ye shall sleep as a slain man sleeps, and the world shall forget you for kings

   .   .   .   .   .   .

   So long I endure, no longer; and laugh not again neither weep.
   For there is no God found stronger than death; and death is a sleep.

Page 67.   Terre Promise

This poem appeared for the first time in Verses; *Dowson submitted it for the* Second Book of the Rhymers' Club, *but withdrew it* (*undated letter to G. A. Greene*). *There is a MS. version extant, in a letter to Victor Plarr dated January* 17, 1893, *formerly in Mr. A. J. A. Symons' Collection* (*S*).

Dedication. *Herbert P. Horne, architect, poet and musician, was founder and joint editor of* The Century Guild Hobby Horse, *which later became* The Hobby Horse, *to which Dowson contributed. Always fascinated by things Italian, he retired to that country and finally died there on April* 23, 1916.

1.) *S:* Even now, the fragrance of her drooping hair *In the letter to Greene* (*see above*) *it is given as* Even now the fragrance of her trailing hair

2. cheek;) *S:* cheek, once,) *S:* once by,) *S:* by

4.) *S:* Then what unsaid things trembled in the air!

5. Always) *S:* Ah, for *corrected* I know, how) *S:* I know so

7. lean) *S:* lean, long) *S:* long, 9. Ah) *S:* Ah,

Page 68. Autumnal

This poem appeared in print for the first time in Verses. *There is a MS. version extant, in a letter to Victor Plarr* (*O'Connell Collection*) *here referred to as* VP; *this version consists of only three stanzas, but in the letter Dowson says he thinks that his muse may in the course of time produce a fourth. Although this letter to Plarr is not dated, we can now place it definitely as* 8 October, 1892, *since it mentions the death of Tennyson, which occurred on October* 6.

Title. *VP:* In Autumn.

Dedication. *Alexander Texeira de Mattos, whose full name was Alexander Louis Texeira de Mattos San Payo y Mendes, was of Dutch extraction, though he was educated in England. He was a translator and publisher's reader. He translated* Pot Bouilli *in the Lutetian Society's edition of Zola's novels, to which Dowson contributed* La Terre. *His high reputation as a translator has lived after him.*

1. Pale amber) *VP:* Pale, amber,

2. October) *VP:* , September

3. sway) *VP:* move
     5. dear! on days like these!) *VP:* Dear! on days like
     these.

8. shadow) *VP:* sunshine   meet) *VP:* meet,
     12. Autumn) *VP:* autumn

15.) *VP:* A little while we have to dream.

The whole imagery in this poem seems to be founded indirectly on that of Keats' Ode to Autumn *and* Sleep and Poetry. *Lines 3-4, before a breeze as soft as summer, has to me a distinctly Keatsian ring, while* dreamful *(12) and* drear *(20) are undeniably Keatsian epithets. How much the two poets thought alike in this matter will be seen from a comparison of Dowson's first stanza and Keats' letter to John Hamilton Reynolds, written at Winchester on September 22, 1819:* "How beautiful the season is now— How fine the air. A temperate sharpness about it. Really, without joking, chaste weather—Dian Skies—I never liked stubble fields so much as now—Aye better than the chilly green of Spring. Somehow, a stubble field looks warm— in the same way that some pictures look warm. This struck me so much in my Sunday's walk that I composed upon it." *(Letters, ed. Colvin, p. 320.) Knowing Keats' poem to have been written towards the end of September, it is interesting to note that Dowson in 12. first wrote September, which, when the poem came to be printed, he changed to October. His own stanzas were composed on October 6th or 7th, Tennyson having died on the 6th; Dowson, from the tone of his letter, writing immediately after, says that the poem was written the day before, when his muse woke after many months' torpor.*

Page 69.   In Tempore Senectutis

This poem appeared for the first time in Verses. *A MS. version exists in a letter to Victor Plarr, dated ca. 26 Oct., 1892. The poem is specifically dated 24 Oct., '92. Dowson was the third poet of the 'Nineties to compose a poem along these lines. The first two were Henley and Yeats. Henley's appeared in* A Book of Verses, *1888, and Yeats' in his* Poems, *1895.*

2. apart,) *VP:* apart;   3. cold,) *VP:* cold: 4. heart!) *VP:* heart,   5. Remember,) *VP:* Remember   6. lingers,) *VP:* lingers   7. sang,) *VP:* sang,   heart, —) *VP:* heart, 10. ancient) *VP:* antient.   11. BE) *VP:* Is   cold.) *VP:* cold: 12. soul's) *VP:* heart's   16. old.) *VP:* old! 18. And every star above) *VP:* And all the stars above 19. Be pitiless and cold:) *VP:* Are pitiless and cold. 20. love!) *VP:* love,   22. us) *VP:* me   23. not) *VP:* now,   strove) *VP:* strove,   24. when I grew old!) *VP:* when I was old!

Page 70.   Villanelle of His Lady's Treasures

This poem first appeared in Temple Bar, *August* 1893.   *No MS. version is known to me.*

Title: *TB:* Of His Lady's Treasure.   (Villanelle.)
7.)   *TB:* "It may be", said I, "who can tell?"
   8. despair?) *TB:* despair."   9. Villanelle!) *TB:* Villanelle.   10. virginal) *TB:* virginal,   11. cheek) *TB:* cheek,   14. tear!) *TB:* tear.   16. musical:) *TB:* musical;   18. well;) *TB:* well: 19. Villanelle.) *TB:* Villanelle!

Page 71.   Gray Nights

This poem appeared for the first time in Verses: *no MS. version is known to me.*

Dedication.   *Charles Sayle was born in* 1864 *and educated at Rugby and New College, Oxford.   For a time after he went down he lived in London, when he was friendly with Dowson. He then moved to Cambridge, where he spent the rest of his life, becoming Assistant Librarian at the University Library.*

1. Awhile)   *Symons prints A while, and at first sight this would seem to be what appears in* Verses; *but a close examination of the latter will show that the W is set solid against the A, from which it seems so far separated because the A is a two-line initial.*

2. No Man's Land)   *It is recognized that this is not an expression coined during the First War; the* Oxford English Dictionary

defines it as an ancient term applied to a plot of land without the walls of London City; the earliest example given is dated 1320. There is also a nautical meaning with which Dowson may have been conversant: "a space amidships used to contain any blocks, rope, tackle, etc., necessary on the forecastle".

Page 72. Vesperal

This poem appeared for the first time in Verses; *no MS. version is known to me.*

Dedication. *Hubert Crackanthorpe was one of the best short-story writers of the 'Nineties. He published three books,* Wreckage 1893, Sentimental Studies 1895, *and* Vignettes 1896. *He also edited the* Albemarle, *a review in which several poems of Dowson's appeared. He lived but little time to appreciate Dowson's dedication, for he took his own life in the latter part of December 1896.*

Page 73. The Garden of Shadow

This poem appeared for the first time in the Second Book of the Rhymers' Club, *1894, p. 105; no MS. version is known to me.*
11. blind) *RC2:* blind;

Page 74. Soli cantare periti Arcades

This poem appeared for the first time in Verses; *no MS. version is known to me.*

Dedication. *Aubrey Beardsley, born 1872, moved in much the same circles as Dowson; they met from time to time in Paris and Brussels. Beardsley also, of course, did the illustrations for* The Pierrot of the Minute, *1897, and the cover for* Verses. *He died in 1898.*

2. Colin) *The use of the name here may have been suggested to him by this line from* La Pucelle, *Canto I, on the translation of which he was either already engaged, or about to embark:*

Colin s'endort sur le sein d'Egérie, . . .

Page 76.   On the Birth of a Friend's Child

This poem appeared for the first time in Verses: *a MS. version exists in a letter to Victor Plarr, ca.* 3 *Sept.* '93.

1. white,) *VP:* white   5. race,) *VP:* race

Dedication.   *Victor and Nellie Plarr were close friends of Dowson, whom he frequently visited.   Victor Plarr was Librarian to the Royal College of Surgeons.   His poems,* In the Dorian Mood, *which should have appeared with Dowson's in a joint volume (see p.* 236), *were issued by Lane in* 1896.

1.)   *It was a Roman custom to mark with a white stone (as chalk) a festival on the calendar.   Dowson, in an undated letter to Arthur Moore, refers to a date to which he is particularly looking forward as:* a day . . . to be ever marked with a white stone.

2. Egeria) *a nymph of Aricia who was courted by Numa; according to Ovid she became his wife.   She was considered by many as a goddess who presided over the pregnancy of women, and as such as she is mentioned by Ovid, Livy, Virgil and Martial.*   *Vide also the quotation from* La Pucelle, *ante.*

Page 77.   Extreme Unction

This poem first appeared in the Second Book of the Rhymers' Club, 1894, *p.* 6.   *There is a MS. version extant in a letter to Victor Plarr (ca.* 28 *Nov.,* '93), *in which Dowson is sending the poem for inclusion in the* Rhymers' Club Book *in place of* Benedictio Domini (*VP*).   (*Now in Mr. Michael Holland's library,* 1946.)

Dedication.   *Lionel Johnson was the same age as Dowson, and a close friend.   Dowson owed much to his clear critical mind.   This dedication is probably the result of Johnson's expressing a strong preference for this poem among those which Dowson submitted for the* Rhymers' Club Book. *He died in* 1902.

It has been pointed out by Miss Katherine Wheatley (University of Texas Modern Language Notes, 1923) *that Dowson was indebted for much of the second stanza to Flaubert's description of the administration of extreme unction to Madame Bovary:* La prête se releva pour prendre le crucifix, alors elle alongea le cou comme qu'un qui a soif, et, collant ses lèvres sur le corps de l'Homme Dieu, elle y deposa de toute sa force expirante le plus grand baiser d'amour qu'elle eût jamais donné. Ensuite il récita le Misereatur et l'Indulgentiam, trempa son pouce droit dans l'huile et commença ses onctions; d'abord sur les yeux qui avaient tant convoité toutes les somptuosités terrestres; puis sur les narines, friandes de brises tiédes et de senteurs amoureuses; puis sur la bouche, qui s'était ouverte pour le mensonge, qui avait gémi d'orgueil et crié dans la luxure; puis sur les mains, qui se délectaient aux contacts suaves, et, enfin sur les plantes des pieds, si rapides autrefois quand elle courait à l'assouvissance de ses désirs, et qui maintenant ne marcheraient plus. *At the same time Dowson did not forget the administration of the same sacrament at the end of* Marius the Epicurean, *and he owes the second line of Stanza I, "all the passages of sense", to Pater. Zola's Le Rêve was a favourite novel of Dowson's, and in this, too, there is a striking description of the administration of extreme unction.*

     1.) *VP:* Upon the lips, the hands, the feet,   *RC2:* Upon the lips, the eyes, the feet,

3. atoning) *VP:* annealing

5.) *VP:* The roving feet that ran so fast feet,) *RC2:* feet
    6. desire,) *VP:* desire   sealed;) *VP, RC2:* sealed:
    7. eyes,) *VP:* eyes   9. free;) *VP, RC2* free,   11.
    life,) *VP:* life?   see,) *VP, RC2:*s ee   12. shadows,)
    VP, RC2: shadows   death?) *VP, RC2:* Death?

13. Sacring oils!) *VP:* healing Oils! *RC2:* sacring oils!
    14. where) *VP, RC2:* where,   when) *VP:* when,
         come,) *VP:* come   15. toils,) *VP, RC2:* toils
    16. you) *VP:* you,   17. Yet,) *RC2:* Yet   18. hour,)
    VP: hour   19. will) *VP, RC2:* shall   20. will see.)
    VP: shall see. *RC2:* shall see!

Page 78. Amantium Irae

This poem appeared for the first time in Verses; *there is a MS. version in BM. Add. MS. 45135 (SS) dated 15 March 1894.*

Title.   Amantium irae amoris integratio est—*Terence, Andria,*
    Act III, Scene 2.   *SS:* Here and Now.

1.)   Down dropped and all the faded roses shed. *Milton,*
    Paradise Lost, Bk. *IX,* 893.   , our rose,)   *SS:* our rose

2. , our days,)   *SS:* our days

4. tempest)   *SS:* shadow

9. *SS:* Or in [our place] appointed shadows,

10. *SS:* Shall [must] hand)   *SS:* hand,

11.) 'a babbled of green fields—*Shakespeare, Henry V, Act II,*
    Scene 3.

11. meadows,)   *SS:* meadows   12. old)   *SS:* old, 13.
    And vainly)   *SS:* And, vainly,   15. love)   *SS:* love
    ungathered?)   *SS:* ungathered,

16. *SS:* The myrtle, never won.

18.)   *It is not unreasonable to conjecture that* Nevermore *came
    into Dowson's mind from Poe's* Raven, *his interest in the Ameri-
    can poet's work being very great.   Indeed, the sentiments of* The
    Raven, *stanza* 16, *are somewhat those of* Amantium Irae.

20. shore,)   *SS:* shore: 21. And)   *SS:* The   22. And)   *SS:*
    The   today:)   *SS:* today;   23. What)   *SS:* What,
    25. Ah,)   *SS:* Nay   30. While)   *SS:* [And]

Page 80.   Impenitentia Ultima
This poem was first printed in the Savoy, No. I, January 1896,
p. 131.   *No MS. version is known to me.*
Dedication.   *Robert Harborough Sherard, born* 1861, *died* 1943,
    *writer, is best known in connection with Dowson as the friend in
    whose house he died.*
        1. ever) *S:* ever,   4. more) *S:* more,   5. "For,) *S:*
    For,   but) *S:* and

6.)   *S:* And that is why I must eat my bread in bitterness and
    sweat;
        7. judgment-seat,) *S:* Judgment Seat   9. "But) *S:*
    But   10. years,) *S:* years;   12. tears.") *S:* tears.   13.
    me,) *S:* me   14. night,) *S:* night

15. light whilst) *S:* light, while   me,) *S:* me;

17. fall and my life) *S:* fall, and my soul
     18. through) *S:* through,   19. Lord,) *S:* Lord!

Page 82.   A Valediction

This poem was printed for the first time in Verses.   *There are three MS. versions extant: one is written on the back of a letter from a share-pusher, dated December 13, 1893 (J. Harlin O'Connell Collection) (O'C).   The second was written by Dowson into a copy of the* Second Book of the Rhymers' Club, *in the possession of Mr. de V. Payen Payne (PP).   Mr. Payen Payne describes how, being together with Victor Plarr and Dowson, he asked both to write in the book: Dowson then wrote out this poem, saying that he had just finished it.   This copy is now in Mr. Michael Holland's library (1946).   The third is in BM. Add. MS. 45135 (SS), and is dated 2 March 1894.*

Title.   *O'C, PP:* no title

 1. part,) *SS:* part:
     2. this;) *O'C:* this.— *PP:* this,   3. heart,) *O'C:* heart 4. kiss;) *O'C:* kiss— *SS:* kiss: 5. say:) *O'C, SS:* say,

6.) *O'C:* Tomorrow or some other day,   or) *PP:* and corrected
     7. part.") *PP:* part" *SS:* part!" 8. weak) *SS:* weak, 9. love) *O'C:* Love   strong:) *O'C:* strong. *PP:* strong; 11. "Life) *PP:* Life   while,) *PP, SS:* while   love) *O'C:* Love   *long;) PP:* long:

13.)   *O'C:* And after harvest God's good time to sleep, *SS:* Or if we reap not, a long time to sleep,— after) *PP:* failing
     14. But) *PP, SS:* And

A. Valediction *invites comparison with Drayton's Sonnet* Since there's no help, come let us kiss and part

Page 83.   Sapientia Lunae

This poem appeared for the first time in Verses; *there are two MS. versions, neither of which is complete; one is contained in a letter*

to Plarr [3 March, 1892]; *and the second is on a loose sheet from another notebook that has survived in F: this consists of the last stanza only.*

Title. *It is an old custom that roses should be gathered by moonlight on Midsummer's Eve by maidens who wish to see their future husbands. Dowson in this case seems to have the custom in mind, and is playing with the idea of finding a new love. The wisdom of the world urges him to go out adventurously, but it is not meet to run for shadows, disclosed by virtue of the roses, when the prize is at his hand. This is borne out better by the Symons MS., and the revisions carry the poem further away from the original idea. S: no title.*

Dated at the end of F: Feb 19. '92.

  2. run,) *S:* run;   20. lilies,) *F:* lilies;   hair) *F: hair,*
  21. laurels;) *F:* laurels: 22. here;') *F:* here.'
  Verses *by way of a misprint omits to close the inverted commas at all.*

23.) *F:* For I had pondered on the rune of roses
23–24.) *S:* This said I, knowing all the rune of roses,
          Which in her hour the pale, soft moon discloses.
24. votaries) *F:* votaries,   discloses) *F:* discloses.

Page 84. Dum nos fata sinunt, oculos satiemus Amore

This poem appeared for the first time in Verses; *no MS. version is known to me.*

Title: Propertius, *Book II, xii, 23.*

23.) Sweets to the sweet: Farewell!—Hamlet, *Act V,* Scene
  I; *this line from* Hamlet *is so firmly fixed in the minds of all who read Shakespeare, that it is not unreasonable to suppose that the shape of his line was brought to Dowson's mind by thinking of it: moreover the following stanza contains an echo of Laertes' lines that immediately follow the Queen's speech as she scatters flowers on the coffin of Ophelia:*
      Hold off the earth a while,
    Till I have caught her once more in my arms:
    Now pile your dust upon the quick and dead

Page 86.   Seraphita

This poem appeared for the first time in Verses; *no MS. version is known to me.*

Page 87.   Epigram

This poem appeared for the first time in Verses.   *There is a MS. version in the Collection of Mr. C. Vincent Armstrong.*

Title.   *CVA:* The Requital   *Dated at the end of CVA:* 29/5/94

The difference between the printed and MS. versions is so marked in its punctuation that it affords a very good example of Dowson's revisions.   As it is a short poem I have printed both versions, for interest, and the MS. reading will be found on p. 186.
6.)   *A reversed Pygmalion and Galatea.*

Page 88.   Quid non speremus, Amantes?

This poem appeared for the first time in Verses: *a MS. version is found in a letter to Victor Plarr, and there dated 9 April 94.*

> 3. slave) *VP:* slave,   5. hours) *VP:* hours,   6. voice,)
> *VP:* voice   dear) *VP:* dear,   9. apart;) *VP:* apart!
> 10. prayed;) *VP:* prayed,   14. last,) *VP:* last;   15. love)
> *VP:* love,   wings) *VP:* wings,   16. soul-centred,) *VP:*
> soul-centred   17. Then,) *VP:* Then   High Love,) *VP:*
> high Lord!   wreathed) *VP:* crowned   19. may) *VP:*
> will

Dedication.   *Mr. Arthur Moore, a very early and close friend of Dowson's, is well known as his collaborator in the two novels,* A Comedy of Masks *and* Adrian Rome.

1. *et seq.)   cp.* Ad Manus Puellae, *p. 20; writers of the nineteenth century Gallic school were undoubtedly lovers of ladies' hands: both Gautier in* Mlle. de Maupin *and Flaubert in* Mme. Bovary *take especial care in describing the hands of their heroines.*

2. women's)   *V: misprinted* womens'

Page 89.   Chanson sans Paroles

This poem appeared for the first time in Verses: *no MS. version is known to me.   The first group,* Ariettes oubliées, *of Verlaine's*

Romances sans Paroles, *contains many of the poems which the French poet's English devotees admired; Dowson's* Chanson sans Paroles *bears striking resemblance to the first poem in this first group;* C'est l'extase langoureuse,

DECORATIONS

Dowson's second and last book of verse, Decorations, *was published by Leonard Smithers in* 1899. *The British Museum date of receipt is* 24 *March* 1900. *There is no* justification de tirage, *but it is doubtful whether any more copies were printed than there were of* Verses; *it was printed by the Chiswick Press. Dowson died so soon after its appearance that it is hardly necessary to add that there was no further edition during his lifetime; it was reprinted from this text in Mr. Arthur Symons' collected edition (Lane,* 1905).

The proofs, corrected by Dowson, exist and are in ·Mr. J. Harlin O'Connell's Collection. They are dated by the Printer 31.8.99. *Apart from a number of interesting alterations of punctuation, by far the most important correction is the change of title. The original title of the book was* LOVE'S AFTERMATH / Poems in Verse and Prose; *beneath which appeared the following lines:*

> Tu mihi sola domus, tu Cynthia, sola parentes,
> Omnia tu nostrae tempora laetitiae.
> Seu tristis veniam, seu contra lateus amicis,
> Quidquid ero dicam; Cynthia causa fuit.

This quotation, which is from Propertius, Book I, XI, 23-26, *was apparently a favourite one of Dowson's, for he added it on what was evidently the title-page of a notebook, later than F, described as:* Fragments / by Ernest Dowson / copied out Paris—to be worked up / Nov, 1897 // *and ascribed it to the twelfth elegy. Of this later notebook only four leaves have survived, slipped loosely into* F: *they contain the MS. of* De Amore.

The cover was designed by Althea Gyles.

Page 92. Beyond
This poem was first printed in Temple Bar, September 1893.

There is a MS. version in F, p. 51.

Title. *F:* To Hèléne - A Rondeau
    TB: A Roundel

Dated at the end of F: Aug 1889. *With the additional note:*
Published Sept 1893 Temple Bar.

1. I think) *F, TB:* ywis   now) *TB:* now,
    2. apart) *F:* apart,
3. saddest) *F, TB:* bitterest
    4. aftermath.) *TB:* aftermath!

5.) *F:* Ay *corrected;* Ah! sweet,—[my] sweet $\begin{array}{l}\text{yesterday,} \\ \text{[erstwhile,]}\end{array}$ *etc.*

    TB: Ah sweet—my sweet erewhile, the tears that start,
    8. Our) *F:* Thy   averted) *F:* Thy saddened
9.) *F:* Our short sweet love is done, we can but part   *TB:*
Our short sweet love is done—we can but part,
    10. reaping) *TB:* reaping,   sow,) *F:* sow

Page 93. De Amore

This poem appeared for the first time in Decorations. *There is a
MS. version on three leaves, numbered 12–14, out of four from a
notebook, that have survived slipped into F. This book was smaller
than F, was of grey paper, and Dowson wrote in it in purple ink.
Its "title-page" has been described, ante. It was obviously in
use later than F: probably following on after the latter was full.*
Title. *F: also numbered (X)*

    3. dies,) *F:* dies   8. awake,) *F:* awake   12. love's)
    F: Love's   great) *F:* great,   sweet,) *F:* sweet   15.
    love's) *F:* Love's   16. defer,) *F:* defer   22. awaken-
    ing:) *F:* awakening;

23. misunderstood discrowned,) *F:* misunderstood *first
draft;* deserted & uncrowned *second draft; this is left and a
tentative* misunderstood, discrowned *written in ink on the
opposite page.*
    26. soever) *F:* so'er   31. star,) *F:* star   34. Love's)
    F: love's   36. miss:) *F:* miss,   38. kiss;) *F:* kiss, *set
    up and corrected in proof.*   40. coronal;) *F:* coronal,   42.

lord!) *F:* Lord! 45. grave;) *F:* grave 46. out-
tyrant death,) *F:* out tyrant Death,

48.) *Dowson had some difficulty in completing this poem. At
the first venture he copied in 1–48 in purple ink, but the hand-
writing indicates that he had to come back to it on two separate
occasions before he could complete the final six lines.*

47. one,) *F:* one *set up and corrected in proof.* 48. sun;)
F: sun, *set up and corrected in proof.* 49. seem:) *F:* seem,
and crucified

50.) *F:* Foiled frustrate and alone, [misunderstood] today
[discrowned]

51. way,) *F:* way

Page 95. The Dead Child

This poem was first printed in Atalanta, *February* 1893. *No
MS. version is known to me.*

1. now) *A:* now, 2. best,) *A:* best; 5. throw.) *A:*
throw!

6–10.) *A:* Thy little life
Was mine a little while;
No fears were rife,
To trouble thy brief smile
With stress or strife.

11.) *A:* Lie still and be,
12. evermore) *A:* everymore, 15. thee.) *A:* thee!
16. deep,) *A:* deep

17.) *A:* I would not *etc.*
18. weep,) *A:* weep; 21. Yes,) *A:* Yea! 22. Dead,)
A: Dead to-day,—) *A:* to-day: 23. said) *A:* said,

26.) *A:* That is the best:
27. child) *A:* Child 28. confessed:) *A:* confest:

29–30.) *A:* I too would come thy way,
And, somewhere, rest.

Page 97. Carthusians

This poem appeared for the first time in Decorations; *there are two
MS. versions; one in F, p.* 77, *the second is in BM. Add. MS.*

45135 (*SS*). *Dowson was much impressed by a visit to the Carthusian foundation at Cowfold in Sussex and wrote about it in a letter to Mr. Arthur Moore. This poem is the outcome.*

Dated at the end of F and SS: 27 May 91.

   2. brought) *F*: brought,   peace,) *SS*: peace: 3. wisdom) *F, SS*: wisdom,

4. release?) *SS*: release.

   5. walls) *F, SS*: walls,

6.) *F*: [only] a sacred silence, [only] as of death obtains; *SS*: Only a sacred silence, as of Death obtains:

   7. here) *F, SS*: here,

9. lands they came) *F*: lands brought here, [ways they came]

ways;) *SS*: ways

10. Each knew at last) *F*: To̞ Each has come [has essayed]

SS: Each has essayed the vanity of earthly joys:

joys;) *F*: joys:

   12. tired at last) *F, SS*: tired, at last,

13–16.) *F: in addition to the printed stanza, has another version deleted; SS has this earlier version, without the deleted* "Still to walk . . ."

Nor theirs to feel the spell of Dominic's holy wrath,
Nor Benedictine ease, nor Francis' milder sway— [still to walk with men beneath sweet Francis' sway:]
Theirs was a loftier calling and a steeper path:
To dwell alone with Christ, to meditate, to pray!

   13. Dominic) *F*: Dominic, 14. gentle sway;) *F*: milder sway: 15. higher) *F*: loftier

17. are companionless,) *F, SS*: are [still] companionless!

   21. gainsay,) *F*: gainsay 23. the) *F*: a

24.) *F*: [For] the sweeter [most sweet] service of the [most] dolorous cross.

   25. last! Surely) *F*: last, surely, *SS*: At last, surely, Ye shall prevail!

28. overcast) *SS*: overcast!

29.) *F:* We $\overset{\text{laugh and}}{\wedge}$ fling up flowers [and laugh], *etc.*

    30. souls) *F:* souls,   art;) *F:* art: *SS:* art!

32.) *F:* $\begin{array}{l}\text{Who dares to say that Death's hard hand}\\ \text{[None whispers that the shadow of death]}\end{array}$ is on his

heart. *SS: carries the deleted version* None whispers . . .

    33. on,) *F:* on   sufficed!) *F:* sufficed,

35.) *F:* Possess your visions still, possess the acting things

    S: Possess your visions, still, possess your aching christ,

36. Surely) *SS:* Surely,   prevail.) *SS:* prevail?

Page 99.   The Three Witches

This poem was first printed in the Savoy, *No. 6, October 1896,*
p. 75. No MS. version is known to me.

    2. dun;) *S:* dun,   5. city) *S:* city,   6. eyes;) *S:*
eyes,   13. We, *S:* We   14. moon,) *S:* Moon,   15.
party,) *S:* party,)   16. soon.) *S:* soon: 18. dies)
S: dies,   20. eyes) *S:* eyes;   21. pity,) *S:* pity

Page 100.   Villanelle of the Poet's Road

This poem appeared for the first time in Decorations; *no MS.*
version is known to me. It was evidently originally written without
breaks, and was so set up, but in the proofs Dowson altered it with
the note: Print in stanzas of 3 lines, final stanza of 4 lines.

Page 101.   Villanelle of Acheron

This poem appeared for the first time in Decorations; *there is a*
MS. version in F, p. 59.

Title. *F:* Villanelle.

Dated at the end of F: 25/3/90 with the added note: Accepted
"Atalanta" Oct 1890

    The Editor of that magazine must, however, have changed his
mind as to the poem's merits after he had bought it, for I can find
no trace of its appearance.

    Although in F the poem is written in separate stanzas, the
copy sent to the printers must have been written straight through;

the same correction had to be made in the proofs as in the preceding poem.

3. scope)   *F: underlined with dots and* set *suggested in the margin.* sun.)   *F:* sun:
    4. one,)   *F: one*   7. done,)   *F:* done—
8.)   *F:* Ywis at last 'tis well, to be *corrected*
    11. ears:)   *F:* ears;—
14.)   *F:* In sleep that wakes not easily.   *corrected*
    17. Persephone,)   *F:* Persephone   19. sun.)   *F:* sun!

Page 102.   Saint Germain-en-Laye
This poem first appeared in the Savoy, *No. II, April 1896, p. 55.   There is a MS. version in a letter, dated December 27 1895, to John Gray. (G).   Dated at the end of G:* Saint Germain-en-Laye.   Dec 1895.
    1. boughs) *S:* boughs,   face,) *G, S:* face   2. close:) *G, S:* close;
3. sullen)   *G:* barren *corrected*
    3. lace) *S:* lace,   5. Say) *G, S:* Say,   7. Oh,) *S:* O, white) *S:* white,   8. sped,) *G:* sped   9. terrace) *G, S:* terrace,   10. laughter,) *G, S:* laughter: thee,) *G:* thee   11. delicate,) *S:* delicate   12. fingers,) *G, S:* fingers;   and behind) *G:* and behind, *S:* and, behind,
13.)   Com, and trip it as ye go
    On the light fantastick toe,
                    Milton, l'Allegro, 33–34.
14. roseal)   *G:* ruddy *corrected*   youth) *S:* youth,
15–16.)   *G:* Have tossed and torn, through all the barren years
            To death, *etc.*
16. death the host)   *S:* Death, the Host

Page 103.   After Paul Verlaine, I
This poem appeared for the first time in Decorations.   *There are two MS. versions known to me.   One in F, p. 80; the other in a letter* [8 Sept, '91] *to Arthur Moore.   It is a translation, in the same metre, of a poem of Verlaine's which has no title: only the Rimbaud*

quotation at its head; it was printed in Romances sans Paroles, 1874 *(reprinted 1887 and 1891).*

Title.   F: From the French of Paul Verlaine.

Dated at the end of F. Sept. 8th, 1891.

    1. heart,) *F, M:* heart   2. town:) *F:* town   5. fall) *M:* sound   8. O) *M:* Ah   10. Fall) *F:* Rain *corrected*   12. hath) *F:* has *corrected*   13. desolate,) *F, M:* desolate   14. Because,) *F, M:* Because

Page 104.   After Paul Verlaine, II

This poem appeared for the first time in Decorations; *no MS. version is known to me.   It is a translation, in the same metre, of a poem of Verlaine's which appeared in* Fêtes Galantes, 1869.

Page 105.   After Paul Verlaine, III

This poem appeared for the first time in Decorations; *there is a MS. version in F, p. 8a, a loose leaf.   It is a translation, in the same metre, of a poem of Verlaine's which appeared in* Romances sans Paroles, 1874.

Dated at the end of F: Feb 92.

    3. Dear,) *F:* Dear!   thine) *F:* my *corrected*   4. awake!) *F:* awake.   7. why,) *F:* why!   9. holly-sprays) *F:* holly sprays   11. ways;) *F:* ways—   12. everything) *F:* everything,

Page 106.   After Paul Verlaine, IV

This poem appeared for the first time in Decorations; *no MS. version is known to me.   It is a translation, in the same metre, of a poem of Verlaine's which appeared in* Sagesse, 1881 *(reprinted 1889, 1893, etc.).*

Page 107.   To His Mistress

This poem appeared for the first time in Decorations; *no MS. version is known to me.*

Page 108.   Jadis

This poem appeared for the first time in Decorations; *there is a MS. version in F, p. 53.*

Title.   *F:* Rondeau *with* Jadis! *pencilled underneath.*
Dated at the end of F: August 24th/89.
 2. celandine,)   *F:* celandine   3. enrolled:)   *F:* enrolled,
6.)   *F:* Your head the sunshine tinged with gold
 8. told:)   *F:* told.   9. Ah, God,)   *F:* Ah God   10.
cold,)   *F:* cold   11. Erewhile.)   *F:* Erewhile!

Page 109.   In a Breton Cemetery
This poem first appeared in The Pageant, 1897, p. 232 (P).   *Three
MS. versions are known to me: one is contained in a letter to Canon
John Gray (G); the second was written by Dowson for Mr.
Michael Holland on the fly leaf of a book at Pont-Aven in August
1896 (H); the third is in BM. Add. MS. 45135. (SS)*
Title.   In)   *P:* On
Dated at the end of P and SS: Pont-Aven, Finistère, 1896, *and
at the end of G:* Pont Aven March/96.
 2. folk)   *G, H, SS:* folk,   anxious)   *P:* stormy   days)
G: days,   3. ways;)   *P, SS:* ways,   4. there,)   *P:*
there   5. long)   *G, H, P, SS:* long,   wave,)   *G, H,
P, SS:* wave   7. well)   *G, H, P, SS:* well,   8. folk,)
H, P, SS: folk   lives)   *P:* life   away,)   *G, P, SS:* away
9. day,)   *G, P:* day;   10. tell,)   *P:* tell
11–12.)   *G:*   Dimly, interminably
                    The same poor rosary.
          H: Dimly, mechanically
                    The same poor rosary.
          P: Dimly, mechanically,
                    Some poor, sad rosary
          SS: Dimly, mechanically
                    The same sad rosary.
 13. falls,)   *G, P:* falls;
14. tempest-tost,)   *G:* tempest-tossed   *H:* tempest-tost   *P:*
passion-tossed
 16. quiet)   *P:* sleepy   calls;)   *P:* calls,   *SS:* calls:
 17. pale)   *P:* wan

Page 110.   To William Theodore Peters

This poem appeared for the first time in Decorations; *no MS. version is known to me.   William Theodore Peters was a young American poet whose life was as chequered and unhappy as that of Dowson himself.   He spent much of his time in Paris, some in London; and created the title rôle in Dowson's* Pierrot of the Minute.

Page 111.   The Sea-change

This poem appeared for the first time in Decorations; *no MS. version is known to me.*

Point du Poldu) *added in the proofs.   Le Poldu is a little south of Pont-Aven, Brittany.*

Page 113.   Dregs

This poem appeared for the first time in Decorations; *no MS. version is known to me.*

Title.   *Originally* Vale; *corrected in the proofs.*

Page 114.   A Song

This poem was first printed in the Savoy, *No. 5, September 1896, p. 36.   No MS. version is known to me.*

5. O,)   *S:* O   10 *and* 15. O, ma mie?)   *S:* O ma mie!
16. pray,)   *S: pray*   20. O,)   *S:* O

Page 115.   Breton Afternoon

This poem first appeared in the Savoy, *No. 3, July 1896, p. 40; no MS. version is known to me.*

1. scented-gorse)   *S:* scented gorse   2. long)   *S:* long,   4. by)   *S:* by,   5. repose,)   *S:* repose;   7. about,)   *S:* about   rose,)   *S:* rose?   8. paleness)   *S:* paleness, ivory!)   *S:* ivory?   9. land)   *S:* World   10. death,)   *S:* death;   11. lie)   *S:* lie,   by)   *S:* by,   an)   *S:* a hole)   *S:* hole   12. deep)   *S:* dark   beneath.)   *S:* beneath.   13. angelus)   *S:* Angelus
15–16.)   *These lines were changed to italic in the proofs.*
15–16.)   *S:* "Mother of God!   O, Misericord! look down in pity on us,

The weak and blind, who stand in our light, and
wreak ourselves such ill!"

Page 116.   Venite Descendamus

This poem was first printed in the Savoy, *No. 4, August 1896,
p. 41; no MS. version is known to me.*
Title.   *S: in inverted commas.*

1. last;) *S:* last: 3. at last) *S:* , at last,   6. mute;)
S: mute: 8. lute.) *S:* lute!   10. and sleep,) *S:* to
sleep,   11. Somewhere) *S:* Somewhere,   13. grows)
S: grows,   15. at last) *S:* , at last,

Page 117.   Transition

This poem appeared for the first time in Decorations; *there is a
MS. version in F, p. 68.*
Title.   *F: none.*

*Dated at the end of F: Dec 26 '92 (90); it seems apparent that
Dowson's hand slipped and the incomplete 0 became a 2; the
poems in this part of F are strictly chronological, and there is
nothing to make one expect a sudden jump of two years.*

1. child;) *F:* child!   2. head;) *F:* head: 3. comes:)
F: comes;   5. thee) *F:* thee,

6. By) *F:* Beside the *corrected.*   bending) *F:* happy *corrected.*
7. and thine) *F:* leave thy   8. Lost in) *F:* Meeting
long and weary) *F:* long, weary   11. through) *F:*
thro'   fields alone) *F:* fields, alone,   12. knowing)
F: knowing,

13–16.)   *F:* Short summer time! and then, my heart's Desire!

The ⎧sadder things⎫ of autumn: one by one,
    ⎩[slow decay]⎭
The roses fall, the pale roses expire
[Beneath the drab reeling of the sun]
[While from the wintry sky there shines no sun]
[Beneath the cold beneath the winter sun]
The sky is desolate; there is no sun.

Pencilled opposite: Beneath the slow decadence of the sun.

Page 118.   Exchanges
This poem appeared for the first time in Decorations; *no MS.*
version is known to me.

Page 119.   To a Lady asking Foolish Questions
This poem appeared for the first time in Decorations.   *There is a*
MS. version of the last four lines among the fragments, *to be*
worked up, . . . 1897 (F2) preserved loose in F.
       9. fall?)   *F2 :* fall   10. blows, Chloe,)   *F2 :* blows Chloe

Page 120.   Rondeau
This poem appeared for the first time in Decorations; *no MS.*
version is known to me.

Page 121.   Moritura
This poem was first printed in London Society, March 1887 *(LS);*
no MS. version is known to me.
       3. done:)   *LS:* done;   4. overhead,)   *LS:* overhead
       5.)   *LS:* (Ah, too soon!)   6. rises, so cold,)   *LS:* rises
       —so cold—   7. winter)   *LS:* Winter   9. gray,)   *LS:*
       grey,   10. fields)   *LS:* fields,   grow)   *LS:* grow—
       14. gaze,)   *LS:* gaze   16. yesterdays,)   *LS:* yesterdays;
       17. Joylessly)   *LS:* Joylessly,   22. stood.)   *LS:* stood;
       23.)   *LS:*— Ah now,

Page 122.   Libera Me
This poem was printed for the first time in Decorations; *there is a*
MS. version in F, p. 3.
Title.   *F:* Hymn to Aphrodite.
cf: Si ab homine malo libero te, prius es liberandus a teipso.
   St. Augustine, Lib. 50, Homil. Hom. 29. Cap. 3. ante med.
   Tom. 10 (ref. Concordantiae Augustinianae, Paris, 1656).
       1. Aphrodite,)   *F:* Aphrodite   2. thine altars)   *F:* thy
       temples   3. send.)   *F:* send!   5. chain;)   *F:* chain,
       7. things I had)   *F:* of my days *corrected.*   my dearest
       and best,)   *F:* with all of my best *corrected.*
8. Fed the fierce flames)   *F:* Fed I the flames *corrected*   altar:
   ah, surely)   *F:* altar:—ah surely
       9. goddesses,)   *F:* goddesses

10. youth thou hast plucked of me,)　*F:* youth hast thou had of me, *corrected.*　　days;)　*F:* days,
　　16. taken,)　*F:* culled; *corrected, retaining semicolon.*　18. go)　*F:* be *corrected.*　21. cast)　*F:* core *corrected.*

Page 124.　To a Lost Love
This poem was printed for the first time in Decorations; *no MS. version is known to me.*
　　11.)　*Proofs:* I know the end before the end is nigh, *corrected.*

Page 125.　Wisdom
This poem was printed for the first time in Decorations; *there is a MS. version in F, p. 48.*
Title.　*F:* This is the Wisdom of the wise.
　　1. spring,)　*F:* Spring

2.)　*F:* [Though] while　wine is red　& spring is here
　　　　　[The while the]　　　　　　　　[and love]
　　　　　[Is not to tired]

　　4. Dear.)　*F:* dear.
　　　　　　[till]
5. while)　*F:* [while]
　　　　　　while

6.)　*F:* Thy dear love
　　　　　The wine grows pale and　*both corrected.*

7.)　*F:* Her flaunting beauty in a smile *corrected.*

8.)　*F:* That who shall　think　of toil and tasks *corrected.*
　　　　　　　　　　　[dream]

9.)　*F:* Dream all thy dreams and dream them true,　*corrected.*
　　　　　　　　　　　　　　　　　　　　　　[well,]
　　9. feet,)　*F:* feet

11.)　*F:* Consume　the bitter with the sweet　sweet:) *proofs:*
　　　　　　[But take]
sweet, *corrected.*

Page 126.　In Spring
This poem was printed for the first time in Decorations; *there is a*

MS. version in F, pp. 29–30. In the proofs there was a dedication to Charles Conder, which Dowson deleted.

Title.   *F:* A Song for Spring Time.
   2. green bedecked)   *F:* decked in green   blithe,)   *F:* blithe;   4. air)   *F:* aire   5. melody:)   *F:* melody—
   7. Cometh)   *F:* It cometh   or)   *F:* and

8.)   *F: first draft:* Mingles the murmur of early bees *revised to:* The sleepy song of the early bees

9.)   *F:* With rustling leaves in the budding trees *corrected.*

10. a gay, blonde head,)   *F:* her yellow head
   13. soul,)   *F:* soul

Page 127.   A Last Word

This poem was first printed in the Savoy, *No. 7, November 1896, p. 87.   There is a MS. version in F, p. 17.   It is the eighth and last sonnet of the sonnet sequence to a Little Girl, the greater part of which was never published: vide pp. 146–153.*

Title.   *F, S:* Epilogue
   1. hand;)   *F:* hand   2. flown;)   *F, S:* flown,   3. sown;)   *F, S:* sown,   4. death;)   *F:* death—   o'er) *F:* on   land,)   *F:* land

5.)   *S has a stanza break here.*   like an owl)   *F:* for $\begin{smallmatrix} \text{every day} \\ \text{all time;} \end{smallmatrix}$
   no choice made.   owl;)   *S:* owl:

6.)   *F:* Laughter or tears, or love, for we have known,
   8. aimless)   *F:* foolish

9–14.)   *F: the sestet in its final version is only suggested by a rough draft on the opposite page:*
                     hence to somewhere dark and cold
      To hollow lands

6–8. *also appear in this suggested revision, which is in purple ink. The original version of 6–14 is a line too long and reads:*
   The meaning of our life, all that is shown
   Surpasseth bitterness: the die is
   [Is bitter to the core, while over] thrown
   The veil of woe enwraps us where we stand.
   Let us go hence, the grave is doubtless cold,

The coffin $\begin{smallmatrix}\text{strait}\\[\text{dank}]\end{smallmatrix}$—yet there just and unjust
Find end of labour, there's rest for the old,
Freedom for all from fear and love and lust—
Let us go hence and pray the earth enfold
Our life-sick hearts and turn them into dust.
9. hence,) *S:* hence   10. Hollow Lands) *S:* hollow
lands,   11. labour,) *S:* labour;   13. O pray) *S:* O,
pray,   14. dust.) *S:* dust!

PROSE

The Decorations in Prose *appeared for the first time in* Decorations; *no MS. versions of them are known to me.*

Page 129. The Fortunate Islands
Paragraph 2: my dreaming) *proofs:* any dreaming *corrected.*

HITHERTO UNPUBLISHED POEMS

With two exceptions these poems are all found in the Flower Notebook (F), which has been described in the Introduction and Appendix II; the two exceptions, which are trifles, and not very good trifles at that, appear at the end of this section. Throughout F Dowson has used ampersands; I have expanded these, as the author would undoubtedly have done when preparing these poems for publication. Otherwise his vagaries of spelling and punctuation have been retained.

Page 137. To Cynara
This poem is written in pencil on the front end paper of F.
9. And I am still thy lover) *F:* ah woe is me I love thee *corrected.*

Page 138. A Mosaic
This poem is written on p. 2 of F.
There is no evidence for supposing that Dowson went to Italy in his later years; his travels rarely took him south of Paris. But

*in 1874 his father was staying at Mentone (R. L. Stevenson,
Letters); Dowson was in all probability with him, and they may
well have extended their travels into the Italian Riviera, or further.*

Page 139.   Requiem
F, p. 5.
*It was a custom of the Primitive Christian Church to place a crown
of flowers at the head of a deceased virgin: St. Jerome, St. Austin
and John of Damascus are authorities for this.   Commenting on*
Yet here she is allow'd her virgin crants, Hamlet, *Act V,
Scene I, Dr. Johnson wrote:* I have been informed by an anony-
mous correspondent, that *crants* is the German word for
garlands. . . .   To carry *garlands* before the bier of a maiden,
and to hang them over her grave, is still the practice in rural
parishes.   *Gough* (Sepulchral Monuments, *Vol. II, Introduc-
tion) wrote:* I have seen fresh flowers put into the coffins of
children and young girls.   *It also became a custom in the
Primitive Church to strew flowers on the grave of departed friends:*
Caeteri mariti super tumulos conjugum spargunt violas, rosas,
lilia floresque purpureos, et dolorem pectoris his officiis
consolantur; . . . *St. Jerome,* Epist. ad Pammachium de Obitu
Uxoris.   *The early Christians adopted these practices from the
Romans, who, in their turn, borrowed them from the Greeks:
vide Propertius, Bk. I, Elegy XVII, and Statius,* Thebaidos,
Lib. X, 782.

Page 140.   Potnia Thea
F, p. 5; dated at the end Aug 1886.
3. Parcae)   *the Roman term for the three Fates, Clotho, Lachesis,
and Atropos; by some they were said to be the children of Anangke,
or Necessity, vide post.*
5. Cronian Zeus)   *Zeus was frequently so called, being the son of
Cronos.*
7. Anangke)   *according to some, the mother of the Parcae.
Dowson has invested her with the attributes of Clotho, the first
of the Parcae, who held a distaff in her hand and was crowned
with a crown of seven stars.*
9. the Cytherean)   *Aphrodite.*

10. Loves) *The L is crossed through and I thought that perhaps* Doves *was intended; but Mr. F. L. Lucas thinks that* Loves *is an echo of the tag in Catullus and Martial* Veneres Cupidinesque.

12. Paphos' groves) *Paphos, the famous city of Cyprus, which was headquarters of the cult of Aphrodite; about a hundred altars smoked daily with continuous sacrifice.*

13-16.) *the city, of course, was Athens. The Delian bark was that which Theseus made, and in which he sailed to Crete to slay the Minotaur; in memory of his success it was sent every fourth year with a deputation to the Delian Apollo.*

21. Olympian queen) *Hera*

22. Hephaestus' fires) *the forges of Hephaestus were beneath Etna; he was the son of Zeus and Hera, or, some say, of Juno alone.*

25. Cithaeron) *a range of mountains separating Boeotia from Megaris and Attica, sacred to Zeus and the Muses. Here Actaeon was torn to pieces by his own dogs, and hence came the first great lion that Herakles slew when still a young man.*

26. Maenads) *Priestesses of Bacchus.*

27. mighty Bromian) *Dionysus, sometimes Bromius, as god of revelry.*

Page 142. Rondeau (I)
F, p. 7.
　　3. the fair and frail) *F: without avail, corrected.*

Page 143. Rondeau (II)
F, p. 8.
The whole is lightly scored through in pencil as a mark of disapproval after Dowson had tried unsuccessfully to get the latter part to his satisfaction; the missing line 12 is indicated with a row of dots and two crosses, in pencil; as he could not find a line that pleased him, he scored through 10–14 heavily, and then, more lightly, the whole poem.

2. still) *F:* dead *first draft deleted;* 　　calm *substituted and corrected.*

12.) Ah sweet howbeit thy heart doth wear *suggested in pencil on the opposite page, but deleted.*

SONNETS

Page 144.   I.   In Memoriam H. C. ob. Feb. 24, 1886
F, p. 9.
I am unable to identify the person in whose memory this sonnet is written; the natural assumption would be Hubert Crackanthorpe, but, even if Dowson had by mistake written 1886 for 1896, Crackanthorpe's death occurred in December, and not in February.

Page 145.   II   Novalis
F, p. 10.
Somewhat like the latter part of Keats' sonnet On first looking into Chapman's Homer.

SONNETS, OF A LITTLE GIRL

This important sonnet sequence consists of eight sonnets, of which No. IV appeared in a magazine and No. VIII was printed in Decorations. *These two belong respectively to Part I, Sections iv and ii; one of them will be found there, but both are printed here also in order that the sonnet sequences may be appreciated as a whole. Personal reasons alone, surely, can have deterred Dowson from publishing more of these sonnets, either in* Verses *or* Decorations, *for they represent some of the best workmanship of which he was capable.*

Page 146.   Of a Little Girl, I
F, p. 11.
   13. calm)   *F: calm, I have removed the comma, which must surely be an error.*
   14.) After Life's fitful fever, he sleeps well;—*Shakespeare,* Macbeth, *Act III, Scene 2.*
   Man's little heart's short fever-fit;—*Keats,* Ode on Indolence, *III, 4.*

Page 147.   Of a Little Girl, II
F, p. 12.

Page 148.   Of a Little Girl, III

F, p. 13.

In this sonnet Dowson made three suggested emendations by writing alternative words in pencil over the top of the original, which is in ink.   Evidently he intended to return to the sonnet and make a final choice.   The suggested emendations are in each case such a definite improvement that I have adopted them in the text; they will be found noted below.

3. hope's)   *F: faith's first draft.*

4. will oft)   *F:* will oft *is actually deleted and* oft *inserted over the top.   This was evidently to receive further attention, since the revised version does not scan and the removal of the auxiliary* will *necessitates the present tense of* relieve, *which would not scan; in the absence of Dowson's final intention, I have therefore restored the original version.*

5. My)   *F:* The *first draft.   An alternative is also pencilled in for* sinking, *but unfortunately it is illegible.*

8. quietly)   *F:* stilly *first draft.*

9. mine)   *F:* my *corrected.*

Page 149.   Of a Little Girl, IV

This sonnet was published in London Society, *Vol.* 50, *November* 1886, *and therefore properly belongs to the next section, but in order to complete the sonnet sequence* Of a Little Girl *and to obviate the necessity of printing it twice, I have put it in here, in its order. There is a MS. version in F, p.* 14.   *It forms No. IV in the Sonnet sequence to a Little Girl, of which the greater part is unpublished. In* London Society *it appears over the initials* E. C. D.

Title.   *LS:* To a Little Girl

Dated in F: 1885   *with note:* published London Society
   1. child)   *F:* child,   3. wondering,)   *F:* wondering
   4. sphere;)   *F:* sphere,   6. storm-tossed)   *F:* storm tossed   7. belongs,)   *F:* belongs   10. tender)   *F:* little tender *corrected*   hand,)   *F:* hand   eyes,)   *F:* eyes   12. loving,)   *F:* tender   replies)   *F:* replies,   13. love—)   *F:* love,

Page 150.   Of a Little Girl, V
F, p. 15.

Page 151.   Of a Little Girl, VI
F, pp. 15–16.

Page 152.   Of a Little Girl, VII
F, pp. 16–17.

Page 153.   Of a Little Girl, VIII
F, p. 17, *and* Decorations ("A Last Word").   *Textual notes on this sonnet will be found on p. 275.*
I have printed it here a second time, in square brackets, so that the Sonnet sequence may be read in toto.

Page 154.   La Jeunesse n'a qu'un Temps
F, p. 18.   *Stanzas* 1 *and* 3 *have something in common with the many palinodes written in the first half of the seventeenth century, particularly that which Quarles attached to the end of* Argalus *and* Parthenia
3. to sombre) to the *deleted.*
12. stay.)   *The fullpoint is omitted in F, obviously by mistake.*

Page 155.   Song of the XIXth Century
F, p. 19.   *Dowson admired Goethe and probably had his alleged last words,* Mehr Licht!, *in mind.*

Page 156.   A Lullaby
F, pp. 19–20.

Page 157.   Spleen
F, p. 20.   *These verses are lightly scored through in pencil; vide the poem following.   Neither bears any direct relation to the several poems by Baudelaire or Verlaine which have this title; Dowson, of course, published a translation of Verlaine's* Spleen *in* Decorations.

Page 158.   Spleen
F, p. 21.   It is evident from the MS. that these and the preceding
verses were written as one poem.   Later Dowson scored through
the first three, which fall on a separate page, in pencil and, in a pen
different from that used at the time of composition, added the title
Spleen *again to the remaining four.*

Page 159.   After Many Years
F, pp. 22–23.
7. old,)   *F: comma added in pencil.*   8. knee,)   *F: comma added*
in pencil.

Page 161.   Praeterita
F, p. 24.   The metre is that of Swinburne's Garden of Proserpine.
38. youth's) summer *deleted.*

Page 163.   Adios !
F, p. (28)*–29.   Pp. 26–27 are missing, and p. 28 is torn out and*
partly destroyed.   At the head of the poem is written (London
Society. March 1887); *as the poem does not seem to have appeared*
in London Society, *this must either have been a note of rejection,*
*or the poem was accepted and neve*r *used.*

Page 164.   Seraphita—Seraphitus
F, pp. 30–31.   The lower half of the page is neatly cut away; it
evidently contained a final and unsatisfactory stanza.

Page 165.   It is finished
F, p. 33.
4. or) and *corrected.*

Page 166.   Ere I go Hence
F, p. 34.

Page 167.   Transit Gloria
F, pp. 35–37.
Dated at the end: May . 19 . 1887.

11.) *F:* Too bitter for pleasure,) *corrected.*

12.) *F:* Too gentle for pain. *corrected.*

14.) *F:* In Vanity Fair, *corrected.*

47. Somewhere) *F:* Far on *first draft;* Somewhere *pencilled above, but no decision made.*

Page 170.   Sonnet, To Nature

F, p. 38.

Dated at the end: Aug. 1887.

Sub-title.   *Well known as the salute of gladiators to the Emperor at the beginning of Roman games.*

3. wild)   *F:* cold *corrected.*

Page 171.   Awakening

F, pp. 39–40.

Dated at the end: May. 1888.

8.)   *Cp.* Transit Gloria, *stz.* 12, *p.* 168.

22. knowledge)   *F:* pleasure *corrected.*

Page 173.   Lullaby

F, pp. 40–41.

Dated at the end: May. 1888.   *There is also a pencilled note opposite:* Rejected—Atalanta.

1–2.)   *cp.*   Blow, blow, thou winter wind,
                    Thou art not so unkind
                    As man's ingratitude
                         Shakespeare, As You Like It, *Act II, Scene* 7.

10. Light up)   hallow *suggested opposite, but no decision made.*

Page 174.   The Old Year

F, pp. 42–43.

Dated at the end: 31/12/88.

25.)   *Between 25 and 26 this line was first drafted and deleted:*
                    Old Year, is it kind or cruel

Page 176.   The New Year

F, pp. 44–45.   *A less certain outlook on the coming year than*

Tennyson's In Memoriam, *CV*.
Dated at the end: Jan. 1889.
9. so very)   *F:* Being passing *corrected.*
10.)   *F:* Will there be one of these shall gain,
11. Ah)   *F:* Ay, *corrected.*
13. Hope not, fear not:)   *F:* Nay, ask not that, *corrected.*

Page 177.   From the Icelandic
F, pp. 45–47.
Title.   *F:* Thalassios *corrected; Swinburne also wrote a poem entitled* Thalassius *in* Songs of the Springtides, 1880.
Dated at the end: April 1889.   *Also there is a note in pencil:* Rejected—Temple Bar
1. Long time ago,)   *F:* When I was young, *corrected.*
5. daedal)   *F:* smiling *corrected.*
12. bitter)   *F:* sad sweet *corrected.*
21. Sea?)   *F:* Sea! *corrected.*
26. Was it not this)   *F:* Nay was't not this *corrected.*   before)   *F:* of yore, *corrected.*
27. Waited and)   *F:* And waited for *corrected.*
31. Ah lean thy brow over me, shroud)   *F:* Ah cover me, lull me, enshroud *corrected.*

Page 179.   Love's Epilogue
F, pp. 49–50; *p.* 48 *is missing.*
Dated at the end: Aug 2. 1889.   *With the pencilled note opposite:* Rejected— English Illustrated, Chambers Journal
3.)   *F:* Dumb *is crossed through in pencil, but no alternative suggested.*

Page 181.   Rondeau.   Hélène
F, p. 52.
Dated at the end: Aug. 1889.
5. What tho')   *F:* Now that *first draft;* Howbeit *second draft, corrected.*

Page 182. Roundel. To Hélène

F, p. 54.

Dated at the end: Oct. 27th. 89.

3. to yearn for them) *F:* to gather up *corrected.*

8. my love and thy disdain:) *F:* the old love that was slain
   —*corrected.*

Page 183. Rondel

F, p. 56.

Dated at the end: Feb. 4. '90

Page 184. Discedam, explebo numerum . . .

F, p. 69.

Title. *Added in pencil. Virgil, Aeneid, vi. 545–6.*

Dated at the end: Jan 31. '91

3. give) *F:* bring *corrected.*

12. On lilies still) *F:* In flowery ways, *corrected.*

14.) *F:* Until the harvest is all harvested. *corrected.*

Page 185. Against My Lady Burton

F, pp. 85–86.

*Sir Richard Burton died on October 20, 1890: sixteen days later
Lady Burton shut herself up in his study to examine all the papers
which he had left. She enlisted a Mr. and Miss Letchford to aid
her in clearing up the effects, but the examination of the MSS. she
reserved to herself on the grounds that Miss Letchford was too young
to see such things. She destroyed all her husband's papers and
diaries, until only the* Scented Garden *and a few others remained.
The* Scented Garden for the Soul's Recreation *was written by
Nafzâwi, a learned Arab Shaykh and physician, about 1431;
the MS. which Lady Burton found was the complete and revised
version, for part had already been published. The contents
thoroughly shocked the righteous widow, but she was prevailed
upon by Miss Letchford to leave it intact. A publisher—perhaps
Smithers—is said already to have offered six thousand guineas for
the copyright, and fifteen hundred subscriptions had been promised.
One night, when Miss Letchford was out, Lady Burton, her mind*

*by no means at rest, went into the study to look at the MS. once
more. She afterwards declared that her husband appeared to her
three times, and thrice commanded "burn it!" Consequently she
did so, sheet by sheet, and the flame of each sheet burning was to
her "a fresh ray of light and peace". In June 1891 she communi-
cated the facts to the Morning Post, and to her dying day was
adamant in asserting that her husband's appearance had been no
hallucination. When Miss Letchford returned on the fatal evening,
Lady Burton, to her reproachful look, said "I wished his name to
be unsullied and without a stain."*

Dated at the end: Nov. 10th. 1891.

17. With deep dishonour) *F:* His whole life's work, *corrected.*
18. With light excuse) *F:* his heart's desire *corrected.*
19. art) *F:* him *corrected.*

Page 186.   The Requital

*The MS. of this poem is a single torn sheet, in the Library of Mr.
C. Vincent Armstrong.   See p. 262.*

6. Turn)   Make *corrected.*

Page 187.   A Letter from M. M.

*This triolet was written by Dowson on p. 213 of his copy of Gleeson
White's* Ballades and Rondeaus, 1887, *which was No. 247 in
the Elkin Mathews-A. J. A. Symons catalogue. It is there
described as translated by Dowson from an unpublished triolet by
Lionel Johnson, which presumably would have been in Latin—
or, ironically, in Greek.*

Page 188.   In the days of the good, gay people, . . .

*This quatrain was written by Dowson in a copy of what must have
been the* Pierrot of the Minute *which he presented with this
subscription:*

> For Miss Ida Baltye
> This piece of moonshine
> With the hommage (*sic*) of the author
> Ernest Dowson

It survives as a loose leaf, torn from the book in which it was originally, and formed No. 209 in the Elkin Mathews-A. J. A. Symons catalogue.

Page 188. In vain we cross the seas change lands, . . .

This couplet appears in F, p. 67; it is crossed through, and now faces the MS. of Little Lady of My Heart, *but some pages are missing and it does not belong to this poem.*

FRAGMENTARY TRIOLET

This fragment of a triolet was hurriedly scribbled by Dowson in pencil on an undated latter to Mr. Arthur Moore and left incomplete. It is included here as an example of his first drafts:

> To think of thee, O death
> How very bitter 'tis
> To him who pondering plies
> His peaceful biz
> To him who peacefully plies
> His   biz
> and battens on his biz

3. pondering)   peacefully *corrected.*

HITHERTO UNCOLLECTED POEMS

Page 191. The Passing of Tennyson

This poem was first printed in T.P.'s Weekly, *then edited by Mr. Holbrook Jackson, in 1915; it was reprinted in the* Literary Digest, *March 27, 1915. The MS. was at one time in the Library of Mr. Edwin B. Hill, Ysleta, Texas, but was destroyed by fire. Through the same calamity very few copies remain of a leaflet which Mr. Hill printed from the MS.*

5. love) *EBH:* love,   9. head) *EBH:* head,   13. world) *EBH:* world,

Page 192. Fantasie Triste

This poem was printed in Known Signatures, 1932. *The*

MS., written in indelible pencil on a single leaf, formed No. 206 in the Elkin Mathews-A. J. A. Symons catalogue. Its interest lies in its being one of the only first or early drafts of a poem by Dowson that have survived.

9. At) *MS:* I' the pale *corrected.* 12. Is all) *MS:* All that *corrected.*

THE PIERROT OF THE MINUTE

Page 193.

The Pierrot of the Minute *was written and performed in* 1893. *The only portion of it that was printed at that time was the Moon Maiden's song, which appeared on p. 4 of the original programme (P), a copy of which is in the Collection of Mr. Arthur Moore. It was not published until* 1897, *when Smithers issued an edition consisting of* 300 *small-paper copies and* 30 *copies on Japanese vellum. It was decorated with a Frontispiece, Initial Letter, Vignette, and Cul-de-lampe by Aubrey Beardsley.*

There are two autograph MSS., both of which are in the library of Mr. Lessing Rosenwald, Philadelphia. I understand that one of them presents most interesting variants.

At various points misprints occur in the stage directions in the form of punctuation placed outside a bracket instead of within it. I have corrected these and considered them hardly worthy of record.

416–440. *This passage has some affinity with:*
        A third interprets motions, looks, and eyes;
        At every word a reputation dies.
        Snuff, or the fan, supply each pause of chat,
        With singing, laughing, ogling, and all that.
                Pope, Rape of the Lock, *Canto III.*

238. rote) *misprinted* note *in* 1st ed. 239. note;) *misprinted* rote *in* 1st ed. 492. Cast) *P:* cast 494. memory,) *P:* memory 496. night,) *P:* night 497. come;) *P:* come, 500. mine;) *P:* mine, 501. thee:) *P:* thee! 504. night,) *P:* night 505. come;) *P:* come,

INDEX OF FIRST LINES